YOGA SONG

Dr. Gregory Ormson

ISBN: 978-81-8253-959-4

First Edition: 2022
Rs. 200/-

ROCHAK PUBLISHING
HIG 45 Kaushambi Kunj, Kalindipuram
Allahabad - 211011 (U.P.) India
http://www.cyberwit.net
Tel: +(91) 9415091004
E-mail: info@rochakpublishing.com

Printed at VCORE CONNECT LLP.

FOREWORD

My entire life has been dedicated to the practice and teaching of yoga. I was blessed to be born into a yoga family, learning yoga from my beloved father who himself dedicated his whole life to the research, practice and teaching of yoga.

In my lifetime, I have researched and read many yoga literatures, sutras, as well as mantras in order to gain a deeper understanding of the essence of yoga. In my yoga journey, I have never come across a collection of yoga poetry. This is both fascinating and inspiring to read. Each aspect of yoga has been covered flawlessly with such details.

Poetry is an art form. Writing a whole book of poetry on yoga is an expression not only of his journey but his deep passion and enthusiasm.

Gregory Ormson is a well-known author, who frequently contributes to the Asana International Yoga Journal. He expresses his sense of humour, admiration for yoga, and love of motorbike through his poetry.

"Yogi, Heal Thyself," and "Release into Savasana" are two of my favourite poems, as they are so inspirational.

It is apparent from the beginning of his writings that he loves yoga and that his view of the practice and discipline of yoga is extraordinary.

I would like to highlight a particular line which stands out to me and shows his deep sincerity in the practice and his deep connection to this practice.

"In the play of yoga, we invest all we are from the inside, here and now. The yoga we are embodying then becomes a defining storyline in our role. We are wise to invest in ourselves now, live it now, and find alignment within self".

- Dr. Yogananth Andiappan

PREFACE

In some ways, I have been writing this book since the spring of 1978 when I first saw yoga asana performed by a man on a dusty, vacant lot in south India. Dressed in bright orange, he appeared to be a *sadhu*, or Indian Holy Man. Crunched into a small, tight compressed mass of flesh I thought he was in pain. I didn't understand. I now know that what I saw was a yogi performing a standing asana called eagle pose, or *garudasana*.

On that spring day many years ago, I knew nothing about yoga, and I could not have imagined that yoga would put its force on me and execute its healing and life-changing work in my life. Yoga's healing therapy on my body, mind, and spirit goes deep; I've written widely of this in hopes that others might open up and consider how yoga will help them in ways known and unknown.

I think of yoga as a song. I find music everywhere and I believe at the center of all time, being, and structure there is a song. Perhaps it's more accurate to say that inside all yoga there is a song. The instrument of a yoga song is our body (which is more than the body); and in every pose, breath, or meditative repose, the instrument becomes a song in motion and in stillness.

Yogi's believed the body is made up of five sheaths or layers (*koshas*). If it's true, when we do yoga asana with our body, we are engaging a physical body in exercise but it includes mind, intellect, consciousness, spirit, and the energy body surrounding the biological shell made of muscle, fiber, blood, bone, and brain.

I use a matryoshka doll to illustrate these koshas and the idea that we are more than what we see. Matryoshka dolls represent the mother carrying a child within. A doll looks, from the outside, like single doll but by pulling the two halves of outer doll apart, we find a smaller doll inside; and then another smaller doll, and another, and another.

We are multifaceted, complex, and unified energy bodies in a physical body. As we look upon one another, we only see one physical body in the practice of yoga asana – the primary focus of my book – but there is more to the physical body and more to yoga that we don't see.

Musicians sense music as a complex continuum of vibration in time. Some musicians and others believe that when playing music they become time itself. During yoga practice of asana, breath, and mindful stillness we are a yoga song in our bodies, and occasionally it seems like we become time itself.

In yoga we are song, and that song is Om (A-U-M). Om is the rhythm and force of the cosmos and our individual lives, and Om is the pulse of the universe's vibration and the vital life force inside the yogi's body that animates all life.

Yoga, both an individual and unique pursuit, is also a corporal event when we practice with others. Everyone experiences yoga from their physical, mental, spiritual, and emotional core, yet the universal constant is that yoga puts us in touch with ourselves and also *something other* than ourselves. It's not critical to me that I locate this something other; I am certain it is present, and I live confidently in the awareness that this something other is always within me, and yet beyond me and outside of me.

I am also certain that defining this something other is unnecessary. My background includes 14 years of work as an ordained theologian and Protestant minister. At one time, I worked hard to define this other that humans call God, divinity, or the eternal; but over the years, my views have shifted and definition is no longer important.

Humans have always expressed a sense of something within, called spirituality, through poetry, music, and ritual. William Wordsworth wrote of it as "something deeply interfused," meaning a presence within. This something is also beyond us and we fall far short of full comprehension and understanding.

In life, I've traveled far because I have strong and deep roots. And while I no longer work in the ministry, my writing on yoga is spiritual in a larger sense of that word. I believe yoga is a spiritual practice. It's also a mental, emotional, and scientifically proven highly beneficial physical practice.

Yoga leads me to breathe in, calming mind and body; and to breathe out, in compassion, smiling. It's my yoga mantra for breathing: a mental, emotional, and physical pattern that forms my breathcentric practice. This mantra focuses my attention and puts me in my body without distraction.

These days, when everyone is distracted, some opening words from *The Yoga Sutras* are entirely relevant: "yoga happens when the direction of the mind is focused and sustained without distraction" (*yogagcittavrittinirodah*). A phrase (or thread of wisdom) like this as yoga counsel could be scripture for the yogi. Patanjali's simple, yet profoundly important instruction is to get present and focus before doing anything. Attention and focus on breath awareness is my guiding principle for both teaching and practicing; it's my roadmap and compass for grounding and living life.

I'm aware that I have blind spots and filters through which I see the world and interpret yoga: Westerner, Anglo, musician, mystic, male, and my life experience as a yogi. This means I need to learn from others on the journey we call yoga. It's a path of discovery in, with, and through our experience alone and with others.

I write as a lover of language in a way that my word selection appeals to me a writer and the sound of words to my ear as a musician. I've formed *Yoga Song* with the rhythm and beat of words in a way that a drummer would choose a beat when finding music pocket. The pocket is the place and time when all the musicians in a band are in sync, and in that experience, both music and yoga hum in pleasing degree.

The rhyme and measure in some places may favor the beat of language over its manifest meaning, yet my deepest hope is to communicate the journey of yoga in a way that is understandable to a reader, and appealing to anyone who hears music in all things.

Long before physicists' established that we are vibrational-beings, or that time collapses and expands as vibrational packets of energy — poets and musicians understood this and they put it in words. Rabindranath Tagore viewed the whole creation as a manifestation of divine music, and wrote in *Gitanjali:* "Ah, thou hast made my heart captive in the endless meshes of thy music."

Eric Schiffmann in *YOGA: The Spirit and Practice of Moving into Stillness*, wrote of yoga as the work of tuning our instrument, "The overall feeling in your muscles and body is the *sound* of yoga. The sound is a feeling, a tone, a feeling-tone; it's very much like singing a note. And if a particular line of energy is not tuned just right, it will either feel "flat" or "sharp." Continual readjustment is necessary to stay perfectly tuned."

American poet Walt Whitman expressed that the body is a song with many melodies when he wrote in *Song of Myself*, "I sing of the body electric." I invite you to listen with me as I step over a threshold and enter the yoga room to tune-up my yoga song and sing out from the depths of the body electric.

I hear muffled sounds from the gathering yogis and my mind is wandering. Soft talk fades into the background; I notice yoga mats stretched out on the floor, and gradually the room becomes silent.

Inside the container of this yoga studio, it feels warm. I open my eyes as the teacher pushes a button to play recorded music. I hear compelling melodies on dahina, tabla, and harmonium from a sound speaker mounted on the wall. Its pours over me like waves from the ocean; it's the nexus of a new identity forming in me.

It starts with small changes. I settle in, close my eyes for a moment, and follow my breath while deliberately positioning myself to receive this unusual combination of Eastern melody landing on my Western ear, reverberating in my Midwestern soul.

My yoga song opens me to sweet release as I mobilize prana, embody asana, and surrender the cares of my restless mind jumping from thought to thought like a monkey leaping from branch to branch. In the heated room, I melt into the floor, and the soft music charms my restless spirit.

We begin with breath in unison, and I follow the groups exhale as the sound of a song generated by each yogi becomes the Om we create together. Centering my mind on my mantra, I go to my practice of breath in calming and body and breathing out in compassion smiling. Following the music within and without, I forget about my agenda for the day as my mind crawls slowly toward a calm shore like a snail over sharp rock.

Time moves steadily and I follow the teacher's directions during an asana sequence. I become time and forget where the hour went. Yoga class is nearly finished, and my teacher tells us to lie down on our backs for corpse pose (savasana). I realize there is no place on Earth I would rather be than right here and right now

Yoga class ends when I hear her voice offer a closing salutation. "May the practice of yoga provide strength to your bodies, compassion and kindness to your heart, calm and clarity to your mind, Namaste." We echo her last word and prepare to depart.

I have a message to share with you: When your yoga class ends, your yoga for living begins. It starts with your electric-body singing your yoga song. You can trust the refrain of yoga's song will always point back to you, where you are led again and again as the song's refrain to tune-up the currents of your electric body.

Yoga song is the sound track to your journey of transformation. It will take you to self-care and open your body, mind, and spirit to wider circles with deeper draws of inclusion. And while I'll never proscribe what you ought to do in your yoga practice, I offer this book as an invitation to listen in on this yoga song; more importantly, I remind you to tune into the song of your electric body and sing your yoga song in your yoga practice.

I'm reminded of something I learned in the desert of Wyoming on my vision quest many years ago. It's not how well you sing your song, but that you do.

Contents

Chapter 1

Yoga as the Sailing Forth

A day after moving into my apartment in Hawaii, I was on the floor with back pain. I had endured many injuries: at 10, I bounced off a trampoline and landed on the ground, a second back injury happened while weightlifting, and yet again in my 40's, I fell from a high roof, landing on a metal ladder.

In Hawaii, I noticed signs for yoga studios everywhere and I started thinking about claims I had heard regarding yoga and healing for back pain. One day, in a desperate attempt to fix my damaged back, and with no background or knowledge of yoga, I decided to try it and hoped to find something to make me strong in my broken places. I feared collapsing in the hot room, but was also confident that if my back held up I would too.

I planned to try yoga for 30 days and then decide if I would continue. I made it through 24 classes that month. My resolve was galvanized and my hope for healing ignited. In my journal entry I wrote, Yoga is the way to go for healing back pain. It's so simple, why don't more people do it? But my transformation from injury to healing went beyond my back as yoga steered me into deep waters. American poet Walt Whitman wrote of such a journey in "Passage to India."

"Sail forth – steer for the deep waters only

Reckless O soul, exploring, I with thee and thou with me"

I continued with yoga and wrote about my experience because I thought my practice in a heated room would also benefit me in other ways. Soon, I was writing on everything that came to me during my classes: I numbered the sessions, made notes about the teachers and their style, chronicled my thoughts about the class experience, and penned other insights that arrived when I was on my mat.

I kept track of the people I met and put their names on a list. After a year I had collected names of 200 people that I considered friends and allies even if I didn't know them. We shared something together and I respected each of my classmates for their courage, persistence, and will. I also watched them grow and marveled at what I saw. The more I talked with them, the more often I heard stories like mine and I learned some of them took up yoga spurred on by a desire to heal unseen emotional wounds.

After a year, I had constructed a personal story of self-recrimination balanced by absolution and inspiration. The arc of my story lifted like a rainbow and I sensed my discovery of yoga's treasures would be at the end of a long struggle. Every moment of trial and endurance formed in me a stronger gratitude and the person I was turning into took me steadily into deeper waters and deeper emotions. I started to care deeply about the important things and less about the peripheral.

Early on, yoga was only a small part of the writing I was doing. Most of it was on family memories, alcohol, education, and the vocational path I had lived. I continued doing yoga and writing, and then after a year when I was emptied by my personal project, and spent of agitation, my attention turned to understanding yoga's dynamic healing energy exchange and what it meant for my being.

Diving deeper, I discovered yoga had become an augury of new life and perhaps a bringer of miracles. Day by day, centimeter by centimeter, my spine was flexed and strengthened, and I welcomed yoga to meet me in a generative engagement. Over time it taught me a reductive mathematic as I learned less is more and offered me a simple yet beneficent covenant. I gave back everything I could.

In the breath-centric expression of my practice, I began mining yoga's treasures and translated them into my redefined biology of belief.

My emotional body was in union with my physical body as I peeled away superficial layers and put my life's vocation and destiny under a microscope. Leaning further into yoga, I experienced its work on me as a timeless process of self-discovery and redemption. Yoga became my transformational container where the inner fire of self-purification (tapas) delivered me to the deeper currents of its curriculum.

The yoga mat became my turf of tears, washing, and regeneration. This was my baptism in fire where I confronted my own life of selfishness and layers of hurt. At the end of class, I kneeled in puddles as sweat fell from my eyebrows dripping onto the towel.

Every tear was made of pain and sorrow for someone I have known and for my sorrow and suffering. I gave to yoga the joys and celebrations of my community; I gave my pain, I gave my heart, and yoga turned me inward to face a new day of healing and redemption.

Yoga did its work on my body and it cracked me open to new emotion. My dream life changed, and a man I had not thought of or seen in 40 years appeared in a dream and said, "Something has changed." It had, and while I was releasing layers of sorrow and failure, I had more to learn; especially how to love myself and my life with my burden of unfulfilled expectations.

Do you want to practice yoga? Think twice, dear reader, because you may find yourself embracing an excavation into the ground of your soul. It's a foray into the unknown and nobody can predict or plan what will be discovered.

When doing yoga, we are on the way to earning a degree in self-awareness. Silence and heightened attention to self in yoga reveals both the vulnerabilities and jagged edges of our lives, but it's also where we come into awareness that we are magnificent in every way.

Yoga is a steady wind and it will push against your sail sending you into deeper waters. You will dance on a road leading to your own soul and this dance with inner spirit-winds (vayus) will lead you to your inmost self, to the authentic you that will challenge the investments you've made.

I never practiced at midnight, but yoga delivered me to something that felt like the midnight hour. The term midnight hour has been used by theologians, seers, and mystics to describe a deep personal encounter where we face up to our inner shadow. It's also sometimes called the dark night of the soul.

I think of the midnight hour as the great collapse. It happens when we come face to face with the knowledge that many of our accomplishments are driven by illusions and fed by self-centeredness. I now realize I was only ignorant. I did what I thought I should be doing and while I was at it, I was like a man pounding a square peg into a round universe.

In your mind's eye, visualize how someone starting yoga is like a graduate at a commencement address in which the speaker is offering advice for the next steps in the journey. They say congratulations for getting this far. They go on to say that your life after graduation will be harder, and then it will get easier, then it will become different, and then become way different. You also hear the speaker say there will be partners to help in your journey after graduation.

Helping partners are those who stand with us and are perched upon the same precipice on which we stand. They are friends that join us looking to the horizon with gratitude for what has passed and in hope for what will be. Your partner is yoga, and it will accompany you right back to yourself, inviting you to do your soul work: opening new emotions, dreams, and memories.

Yoga led me to recall and celebrate who I was and from where I came. I learned how to accept myself for my mistakes, to celebrate my history, and to give thanks for it. When yoga took me to the midnight hour I sincerely felt my sorrow in broken family ties and the anger of my children.

I had been much harder on myself than they were, but as yoga led me past the midnight hour and into newness found through relinquishment, I came to a different place. It was the journey after graduation and it was way different; I was at peace with my life's unfulfilled expectations.

My yoga journey is not obsessive but I'm traveling deep in the waterline. It's a discipline that I enjoy and I move through it with ease. I find sitting in meditation a challenging but regular part of life, and I work to be true to my word. When it comes to resting in yoga, I am completely at peace and in those moments of peace and relinquishment, there is nowhere I'd rather be.

Yoga opened my heart. I listened and realized that I only want to serve. This is the great gift my yoga partner has given as it accompanied me through practice in the morning, in the afternoon, and through the midnight hour.

Be brave and dive deep yogis. The revolution of soul that we willingly embody takes us to compassion, which leads us to transform the world and ourselves. Your yoga partner invites you to continue the journey where it becomes, in time, way different. I fold my hands at my heart and salute you.

Chapter 2

Om

Lyrics from "Woodstock" by Joni Mitchell suggest that we are made of cosmic energy and matter. "We are stardust, we are golden, we are billion-year old carbon . . ." We seldom hear such grandiose and luminous words to describe our being, but when we yoga we are just that, shining and grand billion-year old carbon participating in a pattern that moves the stars and positions us to touch an inner Om at the core of our being.

In a soft chant of Om, rooted and expressed from the core, our cares are set free allowing us to take notice of our deepest truth: we are beings at one with a divinely animated critical mass of stardust and carbon waiting to greet, meet, and welcome us home.

Cultural voices bombard us with a cacophony of dismissal, a poisonous milieu designed to make us feel small and inadequate. News and current events can leave us thinking we're an insignificant cog in a great drama that's happening elsewhere. But to trade our identity as golden children imbued with cosmic energy and force for anything else is a trade down.

Yoga has taught many of us to stop grasping for unimportant things. We've learned that when we grasp for more of what we think we want, we end up exerting a stranglehold and fall out of alignment with ourselves. Alignment with self means we are connected to the core and connected to life, and the sooner we stop reaching or grasping for some artificial cipher of happiness, the more we'll lean into our experiential yoga moments, and let our minds rest in those moments. This is how we learn to ignore the critical cultural disassembly shaping our societal dialogue telling us we are not important.

It's easy to accept that we must pay attention to outer things as a way to participate in life's journey, and to a degree, that is true; but yoga challenges all of our values with a roadmap that's singular in its direction. It takes us to the seat of Om, to the core of our inner self. This core is our full reality in the spectrum we can navigate, and at the same time, it is the sacred self here and now.

From our center of reality and sacred space — Om — we participate in life's journey. Early traditions of yoga named this place of intimate connection with self as "primordial consciousness."

"All the world's a stage, and all the men and women merely players," Shakespeare wrote. And for each of us, there's no play more important than the one in which we participate. In the play of yoga, we invest from the inside, and the yoga we embody during our brief role on the stage of life then becomes a defining storyline. We are wise to invest in our yoga now.

Once we discover yoga's song renews us and helps us inherit fully the moments of our lives, the more we will want to yoga. When observing children and adults, it becomes obvious that adults have lost their spontaneous, joyful ability to live-in-the moment. Somewhere along the way, our freedom and joy took flight when we traded our truest selves — luminous stardust and sacred beings — for the false narratives that dim the light and joy of our being.

Most of us realize yoga conducts a therapeutic alignment within us. Our actions, our emotions, and our thoughts are cleansed and rewritten. Carl Jung once called yoga a process of "psychic hygiene."

Yoga gives us a chance to find this luminous being by focusing attention on the inner Om. It's not a new idea. Russill Paul wrote in *The Yoga of Sound*: "Meditation on the Om offers us the direct awareness that everything in the universe is held in existence by the Divine breath."

Creating the sound of Om and meditating on its meaning invites us to experience this divine breath that the Hebrews called *ruah,* the

Greeks *pneuma,* and the yogis call *prana*. In the moment of Om, divine breath pauses our strategic and analytical brain while firing the existential and experiential brain.

When we chant Om, we may discover that the only thing missing has been our awareness that we are living embodiments to the truth of Mitchell's words; we're beings made of stardust, formed in spirit, animated by breath, joyful and spontaneous at heart.

As we do yoga in motion with quiet attention, or sit in stillness and ease, we come to embody the counsel of its ethics; as we do yoga, we take its wisdom into our bodies and minds where we find sacred self in the depths of our nature. Yoga counsels us to move there in firmness and ease while teaching us to be present in each moment's experience.

There, in the great quieting and stilling of mind and body, we come face-to-face with a golden child. In the chant of Om, we step away from distractions to find a livable balance between the business of the world in which we must engage, and the song of yoga and its compelling melody taking us home to contentment.

The directions to get home are clear: First, slow down and breathe; then focus attention while the mind steadies into a concentrated gaze; and finally, at the end of practice, we may take a moment to come home to self.

Coming home, some will chant the sonorous Om of creation, others may vocalize a heartfelt Namaste, some may sing their yoga song in their asana and in their own way, and for some a silent song of the heart will rise from a meditative place of deep consciousness.

This is yoga's song, arising within the body electric in a primordial consciousness both unique and universal. The luminous, internal Om is the well-trod path providing yogis with something the broken world cannot; the deep, abiding peace of coming home.

Chapter 3

Melody of Motion

When listening to music they love, people sometimes spontaneously get up and move.

When I started yoga, I got up to move and yoga knocked me off my feet and tumbled me like a great wave. My body became a melody in my asana and I responded in movement.

Over time, I learned to trust yoga's curriculum of gravity and heat. Gravity and heat are the most honest teachers I've ever had; gravity and heat are the center and starter to every lesson in asana, every movement of body, mind, and spirit.

In a melody of motion, balanced by stillness, I open to gravity's shaping no matter how I fail. I do yoga linked to breath in the moment. When I'm prepared, yoga shapes me to receptivity where I willingly receive it as an augury of a new song, a blend of stillness, movement, and mindfulness, generated by asana and meditation.

I stay with yoga because l have faith that by working my beautiful, yet wounded human project, I will discover some missing link; some balm of body and mind taught by a messenger from another plane leading me to have faith in the practice.

The faith I hold is unfettered by a particular religious outlook; rather, its my trust in the power of being and the potentiality for living a generative life. When practicing yoga, both meditatively and physically, its song works to empty my ego and prepare me as a vessel for filling and transformation.

It's the song getting into my bones and my response is to do asana and balance this motion with stillness. Each song has its quiet moment, its repose where silence and space become part of the song. It is this way with yoga; in the stillness is the dance, and its at the center of every song.

The best songs include moments of quiet and space between the notes. Beethoven is credited with having said, "it's not just the notes, it's the space between the notes." Providing moments of rest is part of yoga's song of the body electric; it's the stillness between the movements. Yoga's moves and its cessation of moves is the vibrational resonance of the body, building, restoring, and alive in ongoing vibration and electricity.

Yoga's song, powered by asana and composed in the body, consumed my failures and branded me with hidden divinity while shaping and re-shaping my ends. In this reshaping, we tune into the song we are making. But yoga doesn't just make a song with us, it opens us and makes us ready to receive a new song. This is the way of yoga's song composition in, of, and through every every asana in motion and stillness.

For many years, I was a simmering fire of ambition and I lived with injuries and a restless temperament. Then yoga's song registered in me, and I followed its rhythm of movement through active practice and into the lullaby of asana. I didn't expect the moment of repose to take me home or take me to my family where I had both joy and pain.

My yoga witness, based on diligent, truthful practice (*pratyagraha)* is that yoga took me directly where I needed to go; and I believe yoga will take every yogi where they need to go for the balm that heals.

Yoga is a profound journey to individual and community transformation. Like every worthwhile journey, the potential of metamorphosis waits at every turn. The yogi's self-care in mindfulness generates this potential and leads to a new song.

Generated by the connection between yoga and my inner imperishable self (*atman*), yoga came alive in within me in many melodies. The composition of a yoga song in the yogi has no shortcuts; there is no one stop formula or fast track method by which the yogi absorbs yoga's song because the lived experience of yoga is composed from threads of grey that become seedbeds for change. And like every journey imbued with a power for transformation, yoga offers a fire for burning and purification.

It's easy to point to asana as the heat for change, but yoga's cleansing fire also takes place in the stilled gaze of your meditation. Yoga fire, the force of change, is present and in our breath, and it shapes our breathcentric core from the first to last breath.

Yogis learn and their bodies twist and turn the threads of truth into their unique tapestry of integrity and honesty where yoga invites every yogi to inherit its promises. When the yogi gives their pain to yoga it teaches how to let it go. It's the pain of simply being on a planet steeped in pain and it's a pain yogis hold for the world. Pain is part of every yogi's soul song, yet the song's refrain teaches the yogi to trust and to pay attention now.

Yogi's give their love for family and friends to yoga. It's easy to see them aching not just from the slings and arrows of misfortune, the lance of gossip, or backbiting envy, but also the suffering that comes from disease, stress, overconsumption, and worry over material goods and money. Yoga is the noncommercial antidote to consumerism, and in yoga we find a balm that heals or a song that soothes. It's not found in the marketplace, but in your yoga.

I live in a country where many people take for granted the idea of three meals a day, and as a result, I too suffer the illusion of plenty and the scandal of waste. But I give my illusions to yoga because there is nowhere else I take this discontent.

This is the core of yoga's economy, a healing exchange for the taking when the yogi is empty enough to receive. After encounter with yoga, our blood is fired in prana and we are renewed and shimmering with the energy of time and energy. I rest secure in this endless exchange of emptying out and filling up.

This is the great gift of yoga, it works in spite of us to bathe our wounded being and caress our pain with the cleansing of an ancient wisdom-science. This science of yoga and our yoga song moves into us, and moves out from us. It's absorbed into the eternal, the cosmic, and the universal.

The economics of yoga are simple: we give and yoga performs the necessary soul dialysis: it purifies toxicity, re-routes negativity, renews body, trims ego, patches flaws, melts worry, takes on pain, renews our hearts and recasts our breath. Yet even with this soul medicine, I practice so that yoga can work the exchange by taking what I give and offer songs that renew my soul.

When I go to yoga, paraphrasing Rumi, I am like a man in a tavern with many wines but without a glass. I keep going back to yoga where I become a reed dipping into a well of fine wind to absorb and drink its fermented wisdom.

Yogis' give their heart to yoga and yoga reveals its truth. There is not a way to "get" yoga, for yoga in many forms *is* a song already present in the heart . If the song of yoga is already present in the yogi heart, the yogi's first song happens by drawing out or excavating dormant melodies.

"Asana is a sacred offering," B. K. S Iyengar wrote, but asana is a sacred receiving too where we receive and embody asana, mobilize prana, surrender our cares, and focus the monkey mind.

Yogi's give their breath to yoga and it teaches them how to breathe deeper, to trust the inhale, the brief pause, and the full release which returns again as part of the perfect exchange for oxygen rich blood. It begins with giving it away.

The yogi gives their worries to yoga along with their failings and shortcomings. Yoga takes our worries, created in our minds, and through asana and its healing song yoga melts these mountainous worries into molehills and teaches us to release into the soothing song of corpse pose. The yogi gives their burdens to yoga, and yoga, effortless and receptive, delivers the medicine found through rest and recovery.

Yogi's give their challenge of living in a flawed world to yoga where we are all subject to injury from chemicals and artificially modified food and polluted water. Facing misdirected aggression and stress, yogis are like all people for everyone finds that the pain of living in a material world registers in our cellular chemistry. We cannot escape the effects of environmental injuries inherent in a post-Industrial, technological world. The all-encompassing brokenness of our world is just that.

Yogi's give their asana to yoga and yoga turns this energy toward soul care. Yoga asana, shaped by the curriculum of sages and shared worldwide is individual and specific to each one while at the same moment, universally for all.

Yogis' give their egocentrism to yoga and yoga does its work to undo the Gordian knot of self-centeredness. When yoga places our ego focus on hold, it may get through carefully constructed walls to heal us.

By giving to yoga and receiving all from yoga by asana, meditation, chant, and study — including the ethical guidelines relating to our attitudes and relationships to both the inner and the outer world (*yamas* and *niyamas*) — our bodies, minds, and spirits grow, reshape, adapt, and become new.

A fluid yoga remakes us, and in that remaking, every unfolding is connected to another. In the song of yoga, we breathe out to sweet release and our emptying becomes a roadmap for breathing in and traveling on. Our yoga song, our yoga journey, and our yoga path may zig and zag but it will go deep and lead us to the place of still waters.

For centuries, philosophers of the *Tao Te Ching* observed how the cistern filled and noted, "water flows to low places." A sign on the door where I practiced at a yoga studio in Hawaii expresses this curriculum of emptying out and filling by gravity and mystery.

"First it will get harder

Then it will get easier

Then it will get different

Then it will get real different."

Yoga thrives in the middle of different and real different, and yet the ritual center (*axis mundi* – the phrase used in ritual studies) of change occurs inside and outside. On the surface, we look nearly the same every day, but yoga — like the bright sky burning away clouds in the morning — plies open our hearts prompting us to change.

Marion Woodman, a therapist working below the surface to touch the depths of self, wrote about this transformational heat and force (*hatha*) in words that accurately describe the yogi's sincere pursuit: "A life truly lived constantly burns away veils of illusion, burns away what is no longer relevant, gradually reveals our essence."

Yoga is an intensive course in illusion busting. My teachers here and now are like gurus (dispellers of illusion and darkness) and reformers. Under their direction, I go back to that first breath; I go back to the child, back to water birthing life, and back to energy gathering in low places.

With reminders from my teachers and gurus, I go back to the heart. I pause and step into new places and follow new beats. There, yoga starts me up in a repetitive commencement until I am strong enough to stand in my naked truth with clarity and without illusion.

When the yogi trains their body to breathe with ease and move in awareness, and when they learn to arrive at the pose – and life – in equanimity, they move clarity, memory, and experience into their electric body, their body of vibration and song.

In this way, yoga's therapeutic moves body, mind, and spirit to complete relinquishment. There, the yogi breathes deeply, and comes to consciousness slowly as the mind expands. The yogi begins asking bigger questions and as their mind poses, a universal consciousness answers in the song of Om.

Post Modern yogis follow lilting melodies written by a long line of gurus. They ate from the garden and connected to source for nourishment of another sort. As golden beings, we breathe and share the universe's movement to completion. Our choice is simple, yet the contrasting possibilities intensify the nature of harmony or dissonance. We can cooperate with the universe and its movement to completion or we can resist.

Yoga practice teaches the yogi how to cooperate with this greater intelligence as it opens a way for us to locate our enlightened path (*dharma*) to alignment. When we follow yoga's blueprint in surrender and cooperation, a brilliance lights up the fiber of our bodies, and if we are willing to empty ourselves, we may be grow like the lotus in mud. In this growth, we become the heartfelt dharma-song composed for us.

When I insert my ego to force my will, I rough cut a subtle curriculum and dim the splendor of melody accompanying me. Learning all the time, I open to a yoga song as a flower to spring, and seek to correct the direction of my inward compass. My compass is pointing me back to the garden with a yoga song, a song that has reconstituted my mission and expanded my heart.

Yoga's song has showered me in wholeness and connected me to strength of body; compassion, and kindness of heart; calm and clarity of mind. Connection to this provides me with a mission statement for the rest of my days.

Through this yoga, a crucible of fire I've voluntarily entered, I've discovered a precious tradition. I believe it's too holy to treat carelessly, or to let fall into rust. It's counsel is to important to handle with ignorance, doubt, or irreverence.

In yoga, I follow the melody and sink into a liminal space that is my container of heat and transformation. I hear a guru speak of easing into yoga's entry point; I listen to the yoga song I'm making with my instrument, and follow the beautiful transformation becoming me.

Chapter 4

A Divine Comedy

A mountain is more than a rock, a river more than a drop, men and women beyond dismissive labels. In reality we're pieces of the divine; and if pieces are part of a larger whole, then we are fractured pieces of the divine whole.

If we accept the idea of nanotechnologies, we are formed from nano-bits of billion-year-old carbon and space dust. Physicists' tell us that our bodies made of carbon are mostly empty inside, yet the mystics, seers, and others have stated for Millennia that we are participants in a grand story that animates all sentient beings. There is something within us that makes us more than a restless -- and mostly empty — ball of matter

Yoga is song and yoga is drama. Each day we take up yoga in a new body, mind, and spirit as the curtain rises for our part in the divine comedy. Day after day in our yoga we affirm our existence in the great act of simply being. If we do yoga with others, we are witnessed, and we witness others in focused stillness, and in their bending, breathing, meditating, and moving. It is an epic play where we — and millions of other yogis — really are the stars.

Yoga bends and extends the energetic and the actual body. During this extension, we align self to collect the pieces of our lives where yoga's great gift reassembles our minds, bodies, and spirits. Yoga then takes us home where many parts of the scattered yogi are yoked together in unity and healing wholeness. How this happens exactly is the divine comedy in which we engage.

When we set time and intention to be present in life or yoga, self-discovery is inevitable and its proof is in today's yoga explosion. In discovery, we unveil our profound participation in an ongoing divine creation. This is the yogi's new identity, part of the good drama of an ongoing process happening today in ways previously unimagined.

Every time we take to the mat, we become willing players in the ongoing drama of creation. Theologians articulate this creative-evolving reality with the term process theology. Yoga, too, evolves as creative process through a physiology that unfolds within and around us with every breath and every motion on the mat.

I love Shakespearean drama, and particularly Prince Hamlet's words in Act 2 Scene 2 of the play that bears his name: "The play's the thing, wherein I'll catch the conscience of the king." Setting up this scene, Hamlet has changed some dialogue in a play set for a performance in the castle by traveling players. He hopes that a shocking scene, hitting close to home, will awaken King Claudius' conscience and prove him guilty of murdering Hamlet's father.

To awaken is to know deep down we are part of a transformation bringing us home to true self. To awaken means that we inhabit nothing of pretense, neither do we adopt the simulation of *(dissimulare)* false emotions.

In yoga teacher training, we had a conversation on ignorance and delusion (*avidya*). It's the yogis belief that our perceptions are clouded and therefore we are not fully aware. Aspects of avidya: ego, want, attachment, fear, and rejection based on discomfort, cloud our ability to see ourselves clearly.

The nature of perception is not just an afterthought in yoga philosophy but a primary tenant. Patanjali, in *The Yoga Sutras,* devotes an entire second section on avidya and awakening the yogi's perception.

Following our discussion of avidya, we turned to the notion that we are pieces of a fractured and cosmic whole and therefore unable to see clearly. If true, it means the human condition is both comedic and tragic for we are bound to our limited perceptions and the experience of separation; therefore, we are bound to be ignorant and objects of gross categorization.

Today I challenge this notion, but I also know we experience the effects of avidya because its built into the play; however, grace and oneness with the divine are also built into the play. And this is the divine comedy; that we protect ourselves with ego, have limited vision, compromised perception, and are unable to enjoy the play or see it fully. But for those whose perception has been awakened, life is comedy, and a multifaceted riddle unfolding in play.

Yoga moves us to awaken. When this happens, our consciousness comes alive and we realize there is no need to put on a false face. We realize and accept that our lives are set within the theatre of a divine comedy.

This awareness opens us to find the peace of surrender, to enjoy life and yoga just as we are. This is the grace of yoga. Yoga brings us to realize that we are fractured and broken, but also unbroken and whole. We come to realize the grasping and reaching will not change the nature of the play or the song we sing.

Once in a philosophy class, the professor gave an assignment to write our philosophy of God. This was not easy. I struggled, and wrote something about the unmoved mover moving the multiverse to its full completion. I maintained that humans choose to resist or cooperate with the divine movement in process. I argued that everyone is part of the movement, and that we are not helpless bystanders but participants in various roles on the stage called life.

Today, I'd add that yoga brings us to realize that we are fractured and broken, but also mended, whole participants in a play for which our stake gives us the right to choose our form of investment. It's divine comedy, filled with grace and humor but also failure and sorrow. Live now in your yoga and sing out now — it only matters that you do it, not how well you sing — the yoga song of your life in all its brokenness and wholeness.

Chapter 5

Making Heroes

Yoga poses flow in ease when I am calm in breath and movement. Arriving at this point happens in time and it includes preparation of the mind by intentionality, focus, and meditation.

Yoga mending takes us beyond the physical where moments on the mat bring us to face ourselves in moments of stress. These stressful moments and learning to release into ease will begin to affect other areas of life too and that's how yoga integrates the physical and mental, emotional, and spiritual aspects of the person.

Every four years, Yoga Alliance in the US conducts a study and publishes it as, "*Yoga in America.*" In the last published study from 2016 (delayed in 2020 because of COVID-19), the Alliance wrote of 37-million Americans practicing yoga, but only seven percent (excluding teachers) have been doing so for more than 10-years. Many teachers are neophytes too as only 38 percent had been teaching (in 2016) for more than five years.

I've always thought anyone practicing yoga is participating in something heroic. I describe a hero with a noun and verb, for the hero is a person, but a heroic deed is what they do: they meet challenges, carry their strength, courage, and focus into their lives.

They learn it's an active step which takes intention and focus. Aware of our brief lives, the hero has already answered the question of whether or not it's worthwhile to live any way other than heroically.

The yogi channels hero, and is actively engaged, even if they appear to be kneeling in rapt stillness. Yogis are heroic because they are not afraid to try, do not shrink from engagement, and are not intimidated by challenges. This doesn't mean the yogi will never fail. We will fail often – and at many things — but our inner mantra whispers like a soft song on repeat: try again, try again.

It's easy to know what a hero is; simply ask yourself who you admire, what you admire about them, and what would you have to do to be like them? This opens up the definition of hero and means heroic lives need not be marked by fame, fortune, or superpower.

One mark of all heroes is their generosity. They offer their gifts to encourage, praise, and affirm others. One of my professors used to say that if you are an older man and not taking the time to admire a younger man, you are wounding him; the same goes for women. But then he also went on to complete the admiration loop by saying, if you are a younger man and not admiring some older man you are wounding them. Encouragement is a big part of heroes' work. Be a heroic yogi and find someone to admire.

Yoga's challenge is unique; it is a confrontation with self, undiluted by competition with another and not distracted by the tools of sport. Yoga's equipment is simple; but yoga's effects are heroic and profound: changed lives, new songs, and changed identities rooted in the courage and will to carry out heroic deeds and see oneself as heroic.

My teachers say yoga teaches us to relax mind and body in the midst of discomfort. After starting yoga, I noticed a heightened concentration and focus in my life. In the midst of stress as when interviewing for a job, executing a U-turn, riding my motorcycle in heavy traffic, or playing music for an audience, I've been calmed by a new energy, a heroic energy that has moved me into ease.

Yoga's roots are anchored in India and its culture, yet modern practice does not require us to master sacred knowledge or esoteric doctrine to enjoy its benefits. Yoga is enjoyed worldwide and is communicated in many languages.

Patanjali summarized yoga as a form of meditation, practical asana, and spirituality. His great contribution, read by nearly everyone in Western yoga teacher training, is a collection of short passages or threads (*sutras*) which summarize yoga as integrative knowledge. It's wise to keep in mind that Patanjali wrote of yoga as a mental and perceptual discipline inclusive of body, mind, and spirit.

After a couple years practicing in Hawaii, I attended my first yoga workshop where the leader provided updates on the physiological benefits of poses and bodily adjustments for postures. But it was in the posture known as camel (*ustrasana*) where his teaching led to insight and change.

Camel pose is a deep backbend into a maximum extension of the spine: its written that improvements from doing this pose include stimulation of the nervous system, flexibility of the neck and spine, relief from constipation, and stimulation for thyroid, and parathyroid glands.

The workshop leader said the deep backbend is a heart-opening pose and reminded us that an emotional reaction to camel pose is normal because the posture can make us feel vulnerable. Pointing to his heart as the organ which should be at the highest position during camel, he may have even said, 'lift up your hearts' when stressing the importance of making one's heart the highest point.

Hearing this, I recalled my days as a ritual and religious leader and I heard my voice chant the phrase, "Lift up your hearts," known from the 3rd Century in the Christian liturgy as the *Sursum Corda* (*lift up your hearts*) the preface to the Eucharistic Prayer.

Following the teacher's directions, I arched back while letting my head hang back. I pushed forward with waist and thighs; pausing to check the tuning of my body, then deepened my pose pushing my head and neck further back while lifting my chest and heart all the while pushing forward with my waist.

From a deep place, the grief and celebration of my life hit me hard and fast: I heard the plaintive notes of an organ; and in my mind I was moving to an old song-chant, yet in yoga it became a new song. I was at an altar chanting. I envisioned Abraham lifting the body of his son, poised to strike a dagger into his exposed heart; but in my body, I was sweating in a Hawaiian hot yoga room becoming an embodiment of camel.

In that deep bend, I felt tears come to my eyes and roll down the side of my face. I forced my gaze to the back wall, eyeballs rolling up in their sockets. My heart was open and poised to receive healing and fresh oxygen; my adrenaline was pumping and my back stressed.

Drops of sweat camouflaged my tears. I was a hero on his knees actively working to know the truth of his story. It was emotional pain coming forth to the surface of my consciousness matched by the physical stress of the moment.

I wanted to come out of the pose and escape but I stayed, and in those seconds, yoga became my kneeling prayer and my embodiment of spirit and flesh. Then I heard the yoga gospel in the word "change," the signal to come out of the pose.

Releasing from camel pose, I realized some of my old pain was still in me but I also felt an ease and release that I had not known deep in my back. This "lifting up," through yoga's camel posture, had become a healing moment; and in that moment, my yoga had become my embodied liturgy of truth matched by a new song of spirit and change for my back.

Today I lift my heart and chant in a new liturgy, a new song. It's a song built on a foundation of trust in the journey. This lifting up is my new song, a yoga heroes song, one that has molded me like a palm tree swaying in strong wind, formed to bend, but not break.

Chapter 6

A Yoga Parable

Once upon a time, gurus from the East left their homeland and took flight to embody a mission. Their purpose was to share a living body of wisdom known as yoga. They traveled across the ocean to the West by foot, horse, boat, and airplane. Their destination was a place called Starland.

Some of yoga's early writings, preserved on banana leaves or scrolls of papyrus, had crumbled away or were eaten by bugs. But the living wisdom of their mission was alive. Inspired by the Vedas, sealed in disciplined practice, and passed on for centuries by oral tradition, gurus pointed the way to light. When they arrived in the new land, a bold vision drove their work. They hoped to awaken the masses with a song for their soul and were confident in yoga's efficacy.

In Starland, gurus taught their students but were confused by them. The Starlanders were tall, they were loud, and they were rich. They weren't raised in the way of yoga and struggled to follow yoga's subtle melody of gravity. They were impatient with slow progress. They didn't read books, had little use for history, and were uneasy in silence.

But the Starlanders were polite, listened to their gurus, and absorbed ancient wisdom and discipline. They were optimists and opportunists and the illusion of freedom fired their imaginations. Their land was drunk on money, yet they quickly adapted yoga's song to their ambitions.

Many of the gurus were overwhelmed by neon lights and a restless, infant culture; some misplaced their prayer beads and lost their way. Their movement grew, but it shape shifted, and soon the gurus wondered what had happened.

The Starlanders believed in engineering and invention. They lived in a land of diversity and creativity and thought enlightenment connected to entitlement. They were fueled by energy drinks, but gross with anxiety and unexamined ambition. The eight limbs of yoga's wisdom twisted in the chaos of postmodernism.

The Starlanders modified yoga's limbs to speed up the work. They applied teaching learned from their gurus, but didn't fully grasp their depth. Many believed the gurus had brought good medicine, and in time, the practice prospered. Yoga songs from the gurus seemed to help prisoners, alcoholics, the sick, those suffering pain, and even angry youth.

The movement became popular, and in time culturally hip. Famous athletes and wealthy celebrities endorsed the practice. Yogis in Starland posed for photographs in elaborate asanas and they adorned the pages of fitness magazines and billboards.

Some of the guru's felt lost and lamented how the mystic heart of their teaching and the chant of yoga's inner song had vanished. They wondered what happened to union with the imperishable self (*atman)* and the universal imperishable self (*brahman*).

The Eastern gurus realized the slow process of yoga didn't work in Starland, and they admitted to themselves they didn't like superhighways, money, or competition. Some felt haunted by peaceful memories of their homeland: gardens brimming with mangoes and birds, a river of salvation for souls, temples of peace and stillness. Some gurus could not hold the center and returned to their homeland.

Other gurus stayed in Starland and lived through the movements' ongoing metamorphosis. These gurus had students, jobs, and food. A few were famous and became unmoored from the ancient foundations. They had landed on fertile soil and started their own teaching, but the Starlanders had changed them and they didn't recognize themselves in the mirror.

One day, gurus gathered at the ashram where someone read a line from a book.

"Life, like a dome of many-colored glass

stains the white radiance of eternity."

In a moment of clarity, apart from the strains put upon them by the Starlander's, the yogis remembered their mission and committed themselves once again to teaching the ancient yoga song.

A curtain was rend, and the gurus began to awaken from illusion. They went back to their yoga and arrived home – once again - at the beginning where they started over and took up their mission from the beginning.

Chapter 7

A Child Leads

A story in the Christian scriptures wrote of a man named Nicodemus. He asked Jesus, “What must I do to enter the Kingdom of God?” Jesus told him that he must be born again to do so. “How can a man be born when he is old? How can he get into his mother’s body and be born the second time?” Nicodemus asked.

Nicodemus’ rational and literal way of thinking couldn’t imagine rebirth. But yogis can imagine it because they’ve experience many born again yoga moments when the unexpected breaks through.

This story is symbolic, yet born again moments for adults happen when they recover the experience of child-like curiosity and enthusiasm. If adults put on child-like curiosity, they may experience yoga with the fresh perspective of a child and in a sense, become born again or born anew as a child.

Some people introduce yoga to their children when they are just toddlers or infants. Most of us learned about yoga in our adult years, and many of us came to yoga in middle or late adulthood. But through observing a young child, I’ve learned what it may have been like to learn yoga at a very young age.

One night, in close company with a 17-month old, I had been inactive all day and I felt the need to move and do yoga asana. I started easily by practicing a few simple asanas on the living room floor trying to loosen my back and hamstrings. When I began stretching my back in child’s pose, the 17-month old child, completely unprompted, came over next to me and took up a position on the carpeted living-room floor. Nobody had ever coached her, but suddenly she struck the pose and looked over me with a big smile on her face.

I couldn't believe it, but what I saw was child-like enthusiasm, her song of response to yoga that arose in her being as naturally as a laugh or squeal of delight. She was not told to do yoga; she was not invited to do yoga, she only observed and then responded in a way that was natural and fun. Taking this lesson from a toddler is how one is "born again."

I thought that was the end of it, a single experience of serendipity - until one night a few weeks later when I was on the floor in easy yoga poses. She took up position next to me and began imitating the downward dog pose (*ado mukasavasana*) with no encouragement or invitation.

A toddler's openness and enthusiasm means they don't distinguish between yoga or weightlifting, and they don't compartmentalize yoga into fitness or enlightenment; they simply see it as something an adult is doing and they join in because it looks fun and natural.

Her actions prompted me to think about my own parenting. I taught my children to ski, ride bicycles, play baseball, and soccer. And while they learned all of these activities, I would have been a better teacher if I knew that I didn't have to instruct or try to make things happen on my timeline. I was learning that I only had to enjoy these activities myself and let my children take the initiative and copy my actions or not copy them. I learned from the toddler that all I had to do was model and then let their interest pave the way.

Through this learning experience, I realized that my practice can be born again by mental and attitudinal renewal. I'm going to keep observing small children to learn how they learn, but from what I have seen first-hand, I know that the example of children will benefit childlike yogis to do what they do:

V' Embody the song (this is fun).

V' Practice when they want and quit when they want.

V' Receive a gift more profound than they can imagine.

V' Release self from the punishing drive for perfection or correctness.

V' Practice and let yoga flow, allowing it to bloom when the conditions are right.

V' Learn by copying what we see others do and enjoy doing so to the best of our ability.

V' Forget about evaluation or comparison; only be fully present to enjoy the moment.

It may not be possible or practical to bring a toddler into a yoga class so that we could observe the fluid nature of their natural movement, or watch how they learn by observing and imitating. But we might be capable of imagining the child within us; our inner child guiding our attitudes to yoga.

Think of the child's laughter and smile when doing yoga as a song we can adopt: This is how a child becomes teacher. Perhaps we could even ask a young child if we could follow them doing yoga; furthermore, what would that child say to us, how would that child look when it modeled us?

Today, people are fond of integrating goats into yoga - why not children? These questions provide ways for each of us to explore what it could mean if we went back to the starting point and looked with childlike curiosity to enrich our practice.

To fully inherit what he wanted, Nicodemus was instructed to go back to the beginning. Perhaps if we did, we would learn that when the master arrives, it might be a child. It might be wise to watch a child, for in them, the joy and possibility of yoga unfolds in a watchful eye and a smile.

Chapter 8

Seeking Treasure

"*Storage Wars*", a reality TV show on the Arts and Entertainment Network, features people bidding on the contents of abandoned storage units. From a distance, they stand outside a unit for five minutes, and then participate in competitive bidding where the winner then owns its contents.

Sometimes they find material treasures: valuable coins, artwork, or rare documents; but their newly-bought pile could just as easily be crates of old newspapers, magazines, and accumulated collections of extra stuff from lives lived in transit. The TV camera follows them searching through boxes, drawers, and unidentified piles in hopes of finding an alluring item to resell for profit.

It's understood in yoga communities that our bodies are the storage units of past experiences, and these may include mental and psychological trauma along with physical injuries. If one practices yoga consistently, it does not take long before they realize they have something in common with the TV treasure seekers; both treasure seekers and yogis will run smack dab into stored accumulations of stuff they need to deal with. In the storage units of our bodies, we may find not just leftovers to jettison, but also emotions connected to memories that we might honor and remember.

Dr. Bruce Lipton wrote in, *The Biology of Belief: Unleasing the Power of Consciousness, Matter and Miracles,* that our physical bodies are repositories for trauma and stress. He cited evidence to build a convincing case that our life histories are recorded and stored in our bodies at cellular level, and used examples to sustain this theory.

All of us hold memories in the physical layers of our bodies. These emotions, and the stress of life, rest in the ganglion and fascia. Ganglion are neuron cell bodies in the peripheral nervous system intertwined with fascia, the thin casing of connective tissue in the body. Yin yoga works deliberately with body gravity to massage and stretch the fascia as the movement into ease calms the nerves.

One dramatic instance is the story of a young girl who was a heart-transplant patient. Following the transplant, she began having nightmares of murder and her dreams were allegedly so vivid that they eventually led to the capture of the person who had killed her donor.

This is a rare example, but numerous experiments affirm the psychological insight that our bodies and the koshas of our bodies are repositories of memory and experience; not only individual memory but also memory of the entire human species. Carl Jung worked a lifetime examining this wider application of cellular and psychological memory, which he called the "collective unconscious."

If our bodies, like storage containers, hold memories there is a good chance some of them may not be helpful or valuable to us and some may be bad. A worthy yoga effort will be quite similar to that of the storage bidders, to search for the treasure and find a way to let go of those memories that are no longer good or helpful while recovering and restoring to awareness our memories that are helpful.

Yogic work compels us to open-up the storage units that are our bodies, retain only the things of true value, and come to terms with the rest. This process of "body psychotherapy" is not always comfortable, just like yoga, but the good news is that it happens in small degrees every time we go to the mat.

After I started yoga, it took six months before memories from my youth started appearing in the daytime hours and in my dreams. I began to write about this and soon I had hundreds of pages of memories.

I found a way to honor all of it by calling it true, remembering them as fully as I could, and then saying goodbye to them. Some of my memories no longer served me and I consciously let them go by burning every page. This was the value of seeking for treasure in the storage bin of my body. I found cleansing in the act of burning and releasing what I didn't need.

When I began my regular yoga practice I noticed early that my joints, skeletal, and muscular structures opened up; and as is with the body, so it is with emotions. Good memories and experiences are there too; but nobody needs to deal with the good memories because they're not buried under clouds of shame or blame; they're not hidden, and they're not stored as tension or strong emotions in our necks, jaws, hips, back, shoulders or forehead.

This is a big learning curve for many as we often compartmentalize education into either/or packages and define what we do as either a physical or mental activity. It's not easy, for example, to integrate emotional intelligence into a physical education curriculum. Yet yoga teaches just this in its curriculum of heightened mind/body/spirit awareness. Yoga is a curriculum in emotional intelligence, physical education, and spirituality.

A yogi truly wins when they empty their storage bins of anything unnecessary and when they eliminate or at least limit the effects of emotional refuse — even if only for a brief time — and if one really thinks about it in the larger picture of yogic consciousness, is there really anything worth storing under lock and key?

When a yogi wins by losing, eventually devoid of clutter and stored trauma, bodies respond more efficiently; the mind becomes sharper and stronger, and the yogi's spirit is refreshed and energized by the emptying-out.

By living in yogic breath and embodied, mindful moments, the yogi gradually releases trauma and unwelcome energies from the past. They deal with emotions lodged in the body that may have grown into a burden.

We cleanse the storage bins of our bodies when we mobilize breath or the transcendent energy of life (*prana*), embody asana, still the mind, and release into moments of clarity which include dealing with clutter and emotional pain.

This is yoga's therapeutic and it teaches us to honor, remember, and deal with pain. By recovering and affirming that which is truly valuable in our lives, we clean out the clutter, affirm and honor the treasure, and grow into wholeness, health, and strength.

Chapter 9

Yoga and the Pure Consciousness of Healing

The yoga world accepts the notion of unified consciousness but it's not talked about. To the general society, it seems irrelevant, but quantum studies suggest that everything is composed of vibrational energy even if we never see it through a multimillion-dollar subatomic microscope.

Physics has opened us to big ideas like the notion of energy as vibration and a not-yet manifest form of matter. Science like this has led many to accept the idea that matter is not as concrete as we thought. Quantum thought maintains that the unmanifest — or the unseen by us — exists and is as real as each of us here and now. The unmanifest is unrecognizable until energy and matter bring it into material form or until the vibrational energy moves it into our visible spectrum.

Yogic philosophy builds on the same idea as physics: Our bodies contain inner vibration and space and that we are made-up of energy; and that our manifest existence in matter also has a parallel in the unmanifest cosmic seat of existence.

Yoga considers this cosmic seat the *(hiranyagarbha) or* golden temple, and marks it as the origin of all creation and the place of every potential. Technically, *hiranya* means golden and *garbha* means womb and is also called the golden egg.

Some yogis know hiranyagarbha as the heart, and some Indian temples designate their sacred center space as the golden womb, named as the location for the unstruck sound of creation. Yogis know it as Om; its vibrational energy is the start and continuation of everything.

This is how healing consciousness moves too, for consciousness and observation of a thing also changes the mode of being in that which is observed. The Heisenberg Indeterminacy Principle is the theory explaining this insight by articulating that it's impossible to observe matter without influencing its actions. And while this principle was developed studying the velocity and speed of quantum particles, it applies to all matter.

The Christian tradition tells a story about friends of a paralytic man and their determination to place him in close proximity to the pure consciousness of healing in the figure of Jesus. The space surrounding Jesus was crowded, so the paralytic's friends lowered his bed through the roof to the floor where Jesus sat. In that space, the presence and pure consciousness of healing deeply affected the paralytic's wellbeing.

Change, for the paralytic, occurred when his friends acted by opening the door of unmanifest possibility. In that moment, the man in need of healing came into the presence of pure healing consciousness.

The Indeterminacy Principle applied to this story interprets this proximity between two energies as an action with an effect. It's much like psychology's notion of transference; the unseen and unconscious movement of energy between two people meeting.

This happens in yoga with mindful meditation, movement, and breath. It becomes manifest in moments when the yogi is affected by the pure consciousness of an energetic state where matter and mind "see" one another and work as one.

Yoga works on the principle of a connected consciousness or spirit (*purusa*) and matter (*prakrti*). In yoga philosophy, life is a blend of matter and mind, the esoteric and exoteric. In *Teaching Yoga: Essential Foundations and Techniques,* Mark Stephens wrote, "According to the original texts, there are three purposes of Hatha yoga:

(1) The total purification of the body

(2) The complete balancing of the physical, mental, and energetic fields, and

(3) The awakening of purer consciousness through which one ultimately connects with the divine by engaging in practices rooted in the physical body."

If the paralytic's healing story was something that happened just once to one person a long and a long time ago it wouldn't matter to us. However, the story of a man or woman transformed by yoga becomes real when we realize that we are the paralytic man, and the paralytic woman; we are the transformed and healed.

Perhaps we are paralyzed by fear, overwhelmed by responsibility, or weighted down by the pace of life; realizing our state of paralysis, fear, or heaviness with life is the first of many steps to healing consciousness.

A second step may require friends to intervene and place one in need in close proximity to new dimensions of healing. The fortunate among us have friends who will lower us through a roof, take us to a yoga class, or lead us into a healing environment of intentionality and consciousness in trust that the door of healing will open.

Friends of those in need will help because they've been opened by a yoga song and came to inhabit a consciousness that takes them to the state and place of receptivity where the pure consciousness of healing changes them.

Opened by a yoga song of the soul, we are only vessels for the pure consciousness of healing. It's not what we've done, but only that we've allowed this energy to meet, greet, and strike up a song in our soul — the yoga song of pure consciousness, the song of healing.

Chapter 10

Yogi, Heal Thyself

Serving others as a teacher, healer, or a therapist is not an occupation for those with identity questions or ambiguity about their life's work. Therapists and healers speak in common threads of their identity and are confident in their calling.

Many healers and therapists also point out that their call comes from something larger than they are, and they know it in their bones. In the realm of healing work, whether one engages from the prepared space of a therapeutic container, yoga studio, or other public arena, the healer's ego must be strong but not big.

In *Light on Life: The Yoga Journey to Wholeness, Inner Peace, and Ultimate Freedom*, B.K.S. Iyengar wrote that the problem of self-healing is especially difficult for those who have achieved positions of prominence. He writes of ego dangers for physicians, therapists, healers, and other high achievers; yet the generative therapist, healer, or teacher deepens their wisdom when they understand they might find their greatest strength hidden within their greatest weakness.

Normally healer types are highly educated, trained, conscientious, and proud of their work and abilities. This is all good but it can also be a great obstacle because healing action starts by letting go of achievements. This is why healers also need help for healing themselves.

Writing on the pitfalls of human pride, Iyengar warns of ego and self-importance. "Considerable achievements also bring in their wake considerable dangers. An obvious one is pride, not satisfaction in a job well done but a sense of superiority and difference, of distinction and eminence."

Healers need a guide because the ego can get in the way accepting help; yet true healers understand wholesome energy paradigms, and they know humility is the path into honesty. Humility and honesty enable the healer, and the yogi, to face their motivations and seek counsel from others. A healing state of mind fosters an attitude of submission, allows one to examine the pitfalls of ego, and opens one to take the advice of another.

To move from a place of high achievement to self-healing is hard because it takes humility. It's also difficult because the place of humility is not a place. If healing meant a locale, it would be easy to go there and get it, but humility is a state of mind.

Therapists and healers know their patients will test them. In order to achieve the larger goal, sometimes the patient, student, or congregant must challenge the healer as a way to find self- healing. In counsel with a healer, someone may cling, idealize, or try to bring the healer down; a wise and mature healer will be able to handle challenges but they will not take pride in doing so.

A healer prepares with humility and builds a strong ego of identity. In practice, it's only a start, for every healer circles around many times to face themselves in the place where all healing starts.

In moments when the healer sits at home after a long day — feeling busted and broken —when they face themselves and come to the point where they want to sit down in the corner to cry and die, any escapist behaviors, credentials, and achievements will not comfort. In those moments, all yogis and healers need guides.

I've known those moments of brokenness; and all my friends and colleagues in the healing professions have known them too. As a young clergyperson, I had to face my escapist behaviors and learn achievements alone were not enough to sustain me. I had to learn that healing was more than knowledge. It meant I had to get out of my own way and accept help from others.

Yoga's strategic reversal for healing is different from commonly held ideas of healing. Yoga healing moves energy from body to mind and spirit. This happy reversal employs the physical self to heal the mental and spiritual self. One example of how this body energy works on the mind and spirit of the healer is through the humble warrior (*baddha virabhadrasana*) yoga pose.

In the humble warrior posture, the yogi's head is down to embody the attitude of devotion or reverence. The crown of the head stretches forward, completely exposing the yogi's neck. The gaze is downcast, as if avoiding eye contact, with one foot forward and one back. Hands are clasped behind one's back and can be stretched toward the sky. The humble warrior is vulnerable to an approach from all directions.

In this physical posture, the yogi is vulnerable, and therefore open to learning about their their need. As a humble warrior, the yogi bows in submission to an imagined superior as one to whom the warrior serves.

This imagined superior observes in the yogi's oblation the defining attributes of the warrior in service: trust, focus, humility, and discipline. The posture symbolizes the complete offering of humble warriors in service to something beyond themselves.

The yogi or therapist responding from the attitude of a humble warrior can create a healing oasis anywhere and anytime. Carl Rogers named this as "unconditional positive regard," and is the key to how the healer heals self. They do so by letting go of pride in expertise, leaning into the art of humility, and offering positive regard to self and others.

There's no need to overanalyze this because healing is an energy thing, a trust thing, a service, and presence thing. Inner healing is not about ego, it's about unconditional - no exceptions - positive regard for all others and Self.

My hope is that when the healer and the yogi needs healing, they have multiple answers to each of these self-care questions:

What shall I do?

Where do I go?

Who shall I talk to?

The yogic parable of the humble warrior embodies a new truth—that healing can be found in emptying the self of ego in submission to a larger divinity discovered in vulnerability.

Chapter11

Tapas

Mircea Eliade, former chair at the University of Chicago in the History of Religions Department, wrote in *YOGA: Immortality and Freedom,* that the Indians in the *Rigveda* called the practice of using heat in conjunction with strident efforts toward self-purification a *tapas.* Eliade also included North American Medicine Men when he described the use of fire and heat for healing, in *Shamanism: Archaic Techniques of Ecstasy.*

Yoga practice in a hot room ignites the fire of tapas and changes devotees in unexpected ways. The work of yoga is about change, and for many, fire is part of the equation. A fire burns up, down, and sideways with ease; and while it's true that one can smother a fire with water or fire-retardant, fire also abates when it runs out of fuel to burn.

In yoga, the yogi is the fuel and tapas burns away what is not necessary so that the yogi comes to balance. Tapas, made from ardor and heat, becomes a fire that heats and burns away superficial layers of our making, opening our hearts and spines.

Tapas and the use of fire was known to the indigenous Medicine Men as holy work, salvation work, eternal work aimed toward the Great Spirit. But perhaps the best work of tapas is burning away the yogi's need to control outcomes and events.

When tapas burns up the old we learn to align self with a new song, a new knowledge, and a new relinquishment. In the ashes of the old, we accept what has passed and we're opened to grace and newness when a new song rises from ashes.

The force of hatha and tapas cracks us open like a pine cone in a fire. There are many seeds in the cone. When they're flung-out from a burning tree by a raging forest fire, they land on the ground where they're trampled upon and buried. Then nature's hatha prepares seeds for growth by heat and cold, sun and rain, dark and light.

In the tapas of my practice, and its link to muscle and sinew, a moment morphs into my tribute for those who have gone before. I'm surprised when I realize that in my commemorations to all previous yogis, I'm happy and truly grateful to be in the heated ardor of tapas.

Tapas opens us up to a healthy life, but healthy lives happen by degree. That's what keeps me going back to my yoga. It's a practice done in faith and executed by degree; it is not blind faith, but a certainty of outcome accompanied by a vision that goes beyond wishes for immediate results.

New Year's Eve resolutions are often made with an eye toward immediate results but without a long-term vision that includes commitment to a future that is different. Not even three full weeks into the New Year, New York University published a story stating that 90 percent of New Year's Eve resolutions are abandoned. It's because changes happen by small degree and over time.

It's not by adding requirements or resolutions that our lives change; it's by subtracting from our lives that which is unnecessary or unproductive. This is one gift of yoga, we learn by the process of tapas to more clearly define what is necessary and leave the rest. This is yoga's counter-intuitive mathematic; its an equation suggesting that discovery and addition happens by negation and subtraction.

Yoga philosophy develops within the ebb and flow of culture, story, and time. It's an ongoing journey of subtraction and addition. Civilizations grow, but they also burn to the ground. This is the key to yoga's tapas, the burning away of that which is unnecessary.

Its efficacy is immediate for healing discoveries happen in the moments of tapas when we hand over to fire anything that no longer serves for our growth and wellness. In the days ahead, when we're burdened by cares to many to count, we can enter yoga and the fire of tapas that cleans, burns, remakes and never lets us go.

Chapter 12

Lotus Rising

Painted on a north-facing wall in a Hawaiian yoga studio, a white lotus appears over a blue background. At the lotus' base of upward-reaching petals, an empty circle was a bulletin board where studio owners wrote inspirational words or phrases every month. Sometimes they used white chalk and other times the words appeared in pink, yellow, or blue.

A white lotus symbolizes an awakened state, mental purity, and heightened spirituality. Buddhism considers the white lotus to be the womb of the world; and therefore, a place of new creation.

Hinduism's most popular lotus symbol is also a white flower, and its significance is linked to Lakshmi, the goddess of prosperity, and Brahma, the creator of the world and cosmic center of all being and non-being. The lotus, growing in mud, is an apt symbol for the possibility of transformation or change.

In that Hawaiian studio, I looked forward to the new phrase or word in the circle at the beginning of each month. I considered it an anchor to guide my mind throughout the class and over the following weeks.

Over time, I read these featured words: alignment, trust, control, inspiration, Namaste, and ignite, but I was surprised one day when the circle at the lotus' base was empty, a silent cipher, and a table rasa of shocking forlornness. After a while, I realized an empty circle allowed each of us to place our own word, thought, or phrase in the middle of the lotus. The word we chose was up to us.

In my next session, I consciously visualized a word on the empty circle and let it guide my practice. I was creating my own mantra and spiritual center there and then. I owned my yoga script and literally claimed what I wanted to raise up from the mud that day.

Much writing in the field of spirituality has to do with this notion of intentionality, focus, and bringing a new vision to life. Wayne Dyer wrote often of "changing our script," and Sam Keen passionately articulated that all of us are responsible for replacing sickening *(iatrogenic)* stories with healthy ones. San Francisco based yogi Janet Stone wrote in one missive, "*Unwrapping Your Gifts, Healing Family Wounds*" that this work is "an inside job . . . not for the faint of heart."

These teachers have done their work and are sharing important lessons with us. When I rise in the morning, go to the studio and see the lotus, I'm offered a time and place to cast my vision, write my script, and form my new creation. When it comes to yoga for health and joy there are as many ways to write that motto and embody that script as there are people to do it because "it's an inside job."

Mary Karr, author of *The Liars' Club*, leaves no doubt that the work is worth it: "It doesn't matter how bleak our lives are, we still fight for the light. I think that's our divinity. We lean into love, even in the most hideous circumstances. We manage to hope."

The truth we've come to know is that yoga opens the heart which allows for a reordering of life priorities and practices. By writing the new script and fighting for the light, happiness will take up residence in the "deep heart's core" and therefore change the yogi. Happiness cannot settle in a heart filled with bitterness, but neither can it stay away from a true heart strumming a yoga song in chords of gratitude.

In gratitude, and with a renewed vision, the yogi makes choices congruent to who they really are and not to the "meaning-making" façade we often project. The lotus with a blank center helps us to remember that anything is possible.

What do you really want? Write it on the lotus wall with your heart while keeping in mind the principles of alignment. If you ask for something outside the realm of your life, or something that will hurt or injure others, there's a good chance your wishes will hurt you.

Doing our yoga is one way to fight for the light of joy, and with every yoga move we make, we breathe into the good. When gratitude finds free reign in the deep hearts core, happiness and joy bypass the negative barriers that can block us and rob us of life. Our yoga script is the prescription for finding joy in this life.

I remind myself that in spite of the surrounding maladies I envision hope and peace. I also counsel myself that the yoga I do is not just a hobby or something to fill up the time; rather, my yoga is the door through which joy enters into an arena I share with a divinity that transforms iatrogenic stories to generative ones.

Step into your practice today with your heart open to yoga's song. In presence and intent, in stillness or movement, and in the knowledge that your script is at your command, write your song in your heart center and on the circle at the base of lotus rising.

Chapter 13

Threads

Life itself is an art, and the best artists know that even the most beautiful work is imperfect. The indigenous people of the American Southwest – *Diné* – known to the English speaking world as Navajo, are famous for their high-quality, beautifully handcrafted wool rugs. People spend hundreds or thousands of dollars to own one.

But wisdom from this tradition has taught the Navajo to weave one small thread out of place into each rug's pattern; thereby working an intentional flaw into the design. By including a flaw, Navajo wisdom acknowledges the fragility, resilience, and beauty in life.

Movement and motion is the heart and soul of every journey. In yoga terms, our life is an asana in which movement into time is beset with flaws and missteps. Yogis will do well to acknowledge, accept, and include their flaws in asana or meditation as part of the beautiful mosaic their lives create. Yoga's healing patterns in silence, movement, or in stillness, welcomes flawed life, the dissonant thread, or the torn spiders' web.

Many come to yoga with their lives dangling by a thread and their coping skills stretched to the max. Perhaps it's the businessman or businesswoman burned out by economic demands and stresses. Another may arrive at yoga with a broken heart, someone else may be tired of the fast pace of urban living, or fatigued with the demands of social media. In our days of global pandemics, coping well in relative isolation is a new challenge.

This is why Patanjali's writing on yoga has become vital reading and study for the modern yogi. At a basic level all of us can commit one or two of Patanjali's threads to memory. We can put the sutras to work for us when we're on and off the mat, integrating these threads while seeking new patterns of living as we both build newness and bind the threads of our brokenness.

The noun thread is defined as "a fine shard of twisted fibers." It's not hard to see the link between this definition of thread and the work of our muscles in asana, as the muscle is also made up of many fine fibers bundled together. Yin yoga tunes into this with its focus on fascia, and the complex, fibrous weaving inside the human body.

One popular yoga book used in teacher training, *Yoga Anatomy* by Kaminoff and Matthews notes: "The skeletal muscle tissue we see with the naked eye is made up of bundles of fascicles. The fascicles are bundles of muscle fibers, which are the actual muscle cells. Inside the muscle cells are bundles of myofibrils." The threads – in theory and practice – offer an untapped arena for the study and practice of yoga.

Etymology of the word thread comes from the Old English braed, meaning pulled through a needle. The modern yogi can take one or several threads from Patanjali and imagine them as bundles connecting breath to body and soul to the world.

The chosen thread guides yogis in this world, but also braids them to a light not of this world. Yoga threads are a light of brilliance, creating a web to encompass all life. This web of beauty allows us to empty our flawed lives into its net where they are absorbed and dissolved.

If you feel like you are unraveling, do yoga and let its binding-up create healing from your unique collection of mistakes and beauty. Our lives are part of the warp and weft of all creation, and all of us are both beautiful and flawed.

Through yoga we learn to honor our lives as luminous artworks, parts of the whole creation's ever-unfolding glorious tapestry, and perfect in our glorious imperfection braided together by muscle and fiber; woven by shimmering chords of light not of this world.

Chapter 14

Yoga: A Breathcentric Community

In the yoga space as student and teacher I'm part of an ongoing privilege and play. I watch yogis fired by heat and cultural restlessness willingly move into asana and observe as they settle into the wisdom of an ancient practice.

I say "inhale" and witness yoga's remix taking place as they root into their asana and arch upward. I offer another caring command to "exhale" as they breathe and fold into a shape that appears to both stretch and compress their bodies.

The yogis before me are blending the force of opposites in their postures by bringing together upper and lower body. In seconds, they release from the pose and I can almost hear their spines exhale in a deep song of relief.

Observing the gathered yogis stretch into camel or cobra, I marvel that all of us are disconnected from living encounters with cobras or camels; yet below the surface, we are all cobra and camel, and every human is a living embodiment of primal, organic movement.

At best, yogis are present for heightened discernment while yoga presses them into a crucible of equal but opposite force and presents them with the task of being at ease in the moments of stress. It's yoga's therapeutic and they are getting it every time they bend, stretch, pause and breathe.

I glance around the room and see the outline of my community. They are becoming new on a daily basis as they take up yoga. They acted on faith to get here, so I act on faith to teach as the practice of yoga meets them with its global and spiritual energy. It takes courage to move beyond cultural stereotypes and do yoga. It also takes courage to teach this ancient, holistic discipline designed for everyone.

As a teacher, I set the route; and when ready, they follow the road home to themselves. Breath by breath, a universal yoga pilgrimage presses them to question their motives and boldly ask "why am I here?" When the question arises, yoga's song takes over and the yogis remember their courage. They stretch into their containers of reform and travel back to the beginning once again.

The sun is setting, and I look to see my yoga students as hopeful; they tiptoe into newness, and sip nectar from an oxygen-rich moment. Western light, partially eclipsed by Earth, illumines their faces with golden rays as they play dead to integrate the last breathing moments of the best previous moments. Alone, quiet, and on the floor, they exhale. On their backs, they release into savasana and become still as corpses decomposing into the ground.

My breathing congregation, burdened with the weight of their years and stories, is made of ordinary people doing the extraordinary. Their bodies hold sacred songs and mysteries. They are royal dancers, humble warriors, cobras, camels, lions, and stony, worn sphinxes.

Stretching into the extraordinary, they become part of the mystery. Within each pose, willing yogis make a beautiful story of reaching and lifting — failing and persevering – its motor is the rise and fall of diaphragm in full breath and its motion is the story of life's ebb and flow. These yogis are my congregation; I call it a breathcentric community and I deeply affirm their right to ask for fuller breath, richer moments, and wider reaches of spirit.

I've brought them here not through charter or an organizational principle; rather, they are here because they believe something is happening. We are ordinary, but our breathcentric yoga turns us to do the extraordinary and on some level, to be part of the mystery.

This breathcentric community is a great melting pot of diversity and energy. They learn from me but remind me that it's all about the breath. They are not deep in repentance for what was, but boldly follow their long and winding road as they ring-out more life from life.

They are unlike the old congregations I use to inhabit. In my old congregations, souls were far too timid to ask for ecstasy — having been conditioned to think they were unworthy or that it was bad — those congregations, a patchwork of private coroners, hungry priests, and rigid elders, formed a delegation of the disapproving. I wilted under the glare of gaunt penitents who could not sing a joyful song or affirm something good in themselves or anyone.

The teachers in my breathcentric communities are not perfect, but they tell me something good, and they invite me to embrace ecstasy and feel the wind in my fingers. Again I hear a teacher say, "listen to your breath." I listen, and find when gratitude lightens the darkness, the goodness of life forms in my heart.

"We go in to go out," one of my Hawaiian teachers said. It's the genesis of a deeply connected personal makeover. Yoga's inward move is the great inversion of energy and attention and its fully accessible to every yogi from the first-timer to the decades-long yoga practitioner.

Corporately and individually, we've been on Earth for a long time, and we know what falling and rising feels like. Aware of failure and success in life, in teaching, in yoga, we listen when a guide addresses us with the courage to be, a courage found within.

With another breath cycle and hold, I sense the crown of my head rising to an unseen sacred net of prana. I remain rooted, as if I am a monument. I follow for several near-transcendent seconds where I become a living, breathing stone. Then I exhale to feel my shoulders slump, setting me at ease.

I go back to an easy breath with more awareness. I stop traveling and arrive home as the teacher's calm words land in my ear. "Let it go;

it's in the past." In that yoga moment, I was a thirsty man who'd been given water. It was all I asked of the day. I give thanks for yoga, for the water givers, and for the breathcentric practice of yoga.

Yoga is soul work deserving of command and care; its lessons have been won through the centuries and are layered in principles unique and universal. Yoga takes form in us, as it has in all yogis from the past in both motion and stillness.

Yoga's song is like all music. It takes its form through practice and consistency. It's the same with my community. By practice, yoked to individual integrity, we gradually turn from being just a group of people into a breathcentric community singing yoga's songs of renewal.

Maybe you are like me, often a doubting and thirsty man. Your days have registered on your body and your spirit is tired. Maybe today you don't want to do what life asks, but you hear yoga speaking words that flow like water from a clear blue mountain spring. Beside you, a thirsty man is dipping his cup into the spring. I raise a glass and drink. Would you like some?

Chapter 15

Endowed with a Longing for Connection

Yoga community in-person gatherings around the world were deeply affected by an invisible virus called COVID-19. The virus, still with us, has intensified the challenge to make important social connections. I've scaled back my regular yoga attendance at a studio; with the threat of a worldwide pandemic, and my aversion to sickness, I'm cautious.

All of us in the yoga community have responded the best we can, and we've learned to use social media tools to stay in contact with others. But we also noticed that while communities established through the World Wide Web were important, they were different.

I was a college teacher and taught online for six years, but it never felt natural to me. I'm still unsatisfied with virtually generated communities.

These communities are happening though, and through them we are connected by a vast unseen network, much like a network of people transferring an unseen virus with potentially damaging effects. Dealing with fallout from the worldwide pandemic we've learned to navigate a new normal and attempted to go on as before. Concerned about the future and wondering what the next trend or challenge will be, it's hard to be present, calm, and connected. But this new awareness of social space is upon us.

Noreena Hertz, author of **The Lonely Century: How to Restore Human Connection in a World That's Pulling Apart*, wrote, "Even before COVID, three in five adults in the US considered themselves to be lonely." She went on to cite examples in Japan where people were committing minor offenses just to be arrested and go to jail so they'd have someone to talk with.

Social scientists tell us we're re-learning how to reconnect after our forced isolation. This shows both the adaptability of the human species and our longing for a healthy life. We could argue that yoga is built to meet this need because yoga teaches us how to reframe the spaces we inhabit.

Reframing yoga space means redefining social distance and seeing it as the possibility for a new sacred space. If this happens, our yoga communities may become springboards for new forms of yoga and life in the present.

It's nothing new, but worth repeating that yoga comes from the word *yuj*, meaning yoke or connection. A yoke can be hard to bear, but today we know better than before that living without connection is perilous to our health and sanity. I don't know anyone that wants their gravestone to read, "Lived a shallow life alone; buried alone in a shallow grave."

Carl Jung was famous for having said that unless a person has a deep spiritual community to which they belong, they will fall victim to the lower denominators of base instincts or even evil.

I don't think humans are destined to fall into evil without a spiritual community, but without meaningful connections, isolation and loneliness can be a slippery slope to desperation and more.

The myth of rugged individualism, a notion that's driven aggressive ambition in my country, really is a myth. We all need connections with others; and that need is so powerful that people will change their identities, alter their most treasured beliefs, or explore far and wide to find a niche or group from which to draw comfort.

Yoga practice with others, or by ourselves, can open us to a meaningful and powerful connections. Yoga practice in community creates space for dialogue and relationship; it lays down a platform for a starting point to all community, and that is our encounter with self.

Perfection in yoga may have been an ancient goal, and to achieve that goal many yogis spent time alone and in isolation; but I don't know anyone with perfection on their bucket list. I've not heard anyone say, "Yea, I want to become the perfect yogi, to levitate, reach ultimate liberation *(moksha)*, and become one with God."

For most of us, its enough to be at ease in the midst of yoga stress while improving our practice of breath and breathing on the way to a better life. From this, we may form new communities, improve our relationships and lives, and start doing things on our bucket lists either alone or in community.

Yoga is about relationship with self, but also about providing space for connection and learning. This was tested during the COVID-19 crisis. If we have eyes to see, perhaps this crisis has given us time to rethink our activities and connections to others; crisis provides time and space, for us to appreciate and understand that we are endowed with a deep longing for connection.

Its incumbent upon all of us to make connections with others in new ways during these COVID years. And maybe the gift of COVID is that we have time to once again let yoga lead us back to self.

Get back to you and the rest will fall into place. Take care of you and trust that connections and community will happen in unforeseen ways opening you to share your yoga song in a new enlightenment of body, mind, and spirit.

We can discover an unseen benefit in the midst of challenges when we reconnect with self and others on a different level; it happens with practice and time alone, and from that solitary space we may lean a new way to leap confidently into the sociality of the future.

And if you celebrate my learning with me, or better yet, get yourself to the mat so that you can learn something new … then I'm happy for you. If your goal is to be perfect, you're welcome to go for it. I'll wait for your video showing me that you've levitated. But until that time, let's reimagine Hamlet's sardonic words to Ophelia. Get thee to a yoga session . . . even if it's just you.

Chapter 16

Yogatecture: Blueprint of Transformation

Yoga transforms lives from the ground up. Many of us started yoga because of the healing inherent in its movements or asanas, and it's the place most of us started building our yoga foundation. Yet even a new student to yoga learns that asana is just one part of yoga's eightfold path to healing and wholeness.

Builders say the most important structural aspect of a building is its foundation. B.K.S. Iyengar spoke directly on foundational work in *Light on Life: The Yoga Journey to Wholeness, Inner Peace, and Ultimate Freedom*. "In each asana, if the contact between body and the floor – the foundation – is good, the asana will be performed well. Always watch your base, be attentive to the portion nearest the ground and correct first from the root. The standing poses are meant to begin providing this foundation for life."

Starting with the foundation, we train our bodies with strong standing postures built on good intentions and conscious living patterns. Standing solid, our foundation is like a tree trunk in the forest, deeply anchored and yet allowing movement in the limbs as they adjust to winds of change.

Asana is also the ground and heart of an embodied spiritual practice because asana is a moving prayer. Many people pray in church, in nature, in a building, or some other religious setting, but these prayers most often exclude movement.

Working as a Protestant clergy, I observed most prayer offerings happened when people were standing still, sitting still, or kneeling. Nobody talked about the body involved in prayer, even though the body is more than just body.

This has to do with the Western philosophical inheritance of a body/ mind split or dualism, and the rough designation that mind is good and body is not good. Contemporary yoga does not accept this split as the inferred *(apriori)* assumption about body or mind as opposite and unequal aspects of the human being.

Prayer without the body misses spiritual embodiment, and if spirituality is not embodied in people, then where is it? We learn in yoga that as we open our bodies in asana, we are also opening spirit, mind, consciousness, and the energy body. When yoga asana, and the practice of meditation open the physical body, all other aspects of the koshas follow; this makes asana an expression of gratitude and a moving prayer: a physical, mental, emotional, and spiritual action.

Yoga-prayers are not asking for something; rather, they are our full mind, body, and spirit response to breath and life itself. "Asana is a sacred offering," Iyengar wrote. He was right, but its a sacred receiving too, where yogis receive the benefits of embodying asanas, mobilizing prana, surrendering our cares, and focusing our monkey minds.

In that way asana is prayer, and this prayer is a yoga song of gratitude for life. This is transformational – because it involves all aspects of the human being — and it's the foundation of yogatecture; its both the blueprint for yoga and it is the work of the yogi.

The yogi builds their sacred dwelling out of their bodies by following a longstanding proven practice. The building takes shape over time as the yogi's practice develops. The yogi's song, created and motivated by gratitude, sustained by truth, and fortified by practice, also takes shape over time. Through earnest seeking, the yogi begins to shine with an inner wisdom constructed by yogatecture: aligning body, mind, and spirit in a sacred and sound dwelling.

When yogi's follow yogatecture as both a practice, and a building blueprint. By following the blueprint we come to build a sacred dwelling with many rooms that are alive with windows, elegant doors and gates, synchronically opening and closing. In the rooms of this dwelling, the yogi engages in ongoing construction where the square angles are rounded and energy freely flows for health and wellbeing.

The process is simple and the blueprint is clear. It starts with one conscious breath followed by another and another. This is how we build a sacred and sound structure. It is the physical, non-physical, and metaphysical work of yoga derived from a longstanding blueprint.

This blueprint includes asana, pranayama, meditation, and observance of yoga's limbs. It provides the yogi with both the tools and the means to build. On the journey, the yogi's tools evolve as the ongoing building compels them to continually refurbish the rooms of their dwelling and their being.

In the rich dwelling built by yogatecture, we are part of yoga's ongoing play and privilege. We see yogi's practicing and we do well to view them and ourselves as heroes engaged in the heroic work of building and rebuilding from foundation up.

Breath by breath, moving prayer by moving prayer, the will to build a sacred dwelling is formed by inspiration in the ardor and heat of yoga aligned with intent. Inside, within their mansion, the yogi's sacred center is animated by self-love and love for others.

Yogatecture is built on the simple principle of yogi's doing yoga; in doing so they inhabit their spiritual center; breathe deep, and drink from the well of wisdom. They embrace each layer greeting them every time they strike a pose, release into savasana, observe a discipline, or pause to collect themselves in the present moment.

Yogis learn through tapas to strip away matters that are not essential (*adiaphora*) to a faithful practice, unveiling the elaborate, yet intimate personal architecture of yoga, a yogatecture. Yogis both give and receive from yoga. In this two-way transference, they learn to respect their house, respect one another, and respect the world while building their dwelling of truth.

Like good builders, they start with the foundation, and then build the walls and roof of their inner mansion. Built in gratitude, the yogi takes breath not just in a house, but in a sacred dwelling, one built by an elegant heritage moment by moment, limb by limb, breath by breath, song by song, and prayer by prayer.

Chapter 17

Transforming the Emotional Body

Louie Netz, former director for Harley Davidson's Styling and Graphics Department once said, "Form and function both report to emotion." When we observe a yoga pose or the stylish symmetry of a Harley cutting a sharp curve, it's easy to believe motorcycles are about speeding through turns and yoga about perfectly executed and aligned asanas.

And it's true that a yogi on the mat and a Harley on the highway perform their function to a high degree. But the power of yoga – like the allure of a great motorcycle – is in its move from high function to strong emotion.

Like many newcomers, when I started yoga I thought it was about what I saw. I noticed people bending into forms that were — at first — perplexing. I also thought it was about what I heard yoga could do for my injuries; at the beginning, that's all I expected.

My yoga education was gradual. At first I practiced to feel better, then to learn good alignment, and then to accomplish more asanas. As a dedicated student, I paid attention to words from my teachers as they led me to correct placement of my feet, my hands, and my gaze. I followed their instructions, which led me through breathing techniques and transitions. At the end, I lay down with other yogis in stillness, like a motorcycle resting on its jiffy-stand.

But right away, I sensed there was something happening well beyond what was taking place in my physical experience on the mat. I didn't know it, but I was on my way to connect deeply to my full self, and at the same time, touch something much broader and deeper than myself. By a gradual knitting-together of mind, body, and spirit as one, I sensed good changes happening and decided to keep practicing yoga.

Yoga is a dynamic leader — both gentle and firm — that invited me to an active role from a passive one. When the yogi accepts this invitation, they wake to a transforming spiral of learning from the inside out.

Preparing the yogi for deep connection to self was originally a long and arduous process of discipline for the mind, body, and spirit. For centuries, yoga progressed by small steps and it continues in this predictable way. Yoga improves mental and physical discipline, increases bodily strength, improves flexibility, improves balance, heightens endurance, and develops muscle tone.

For the early yogis, and for us, a beneficial practical step was cerebral. The yogi engaged in mental training and meditation, breath-work, and studied the ethics concerning inner and outer life. Mental yoga improves concentration and connects the yogi with more awareness to life's physical and metaphysical relationships and spaces. The modern yogi will grow to understand yoga is at once a physical, non-physical, and meta-physical process that works on his or her entire being.

Yogis today find new challenges, but most of us, unlike yogis of old forego seeking answers from our individual gurus; rather, we tune into our experience, which becomes our guiding beacon. Many seek support from therapists or counselors, but in the West, I've never heard of anyone going to their guru for advice on important life decisions.

The yoga journey is often an emotional road. Teachers may say at the start of a pose, "This might bring something up in you." That something could be any person, place, or event from the yogi's past that hurt, limited, rejected or doubted them. This is the beginning of yoga's emotional rescue and an apt illustration of how the form and function of yoga connect to emotion. If one is aware of their emotional body through meditation, journaling, or deep reflection, yoga will put them directly in touch with emotional awareness.

When I began the practice, I became aware of tension from my professional and intellectual work stored in my shoulders. Through awareness of the emotional body my practice taught me that this tension is aligned most closely – though not solely — with jealousy. Further energetic therapy for this would have me attend to the throat chakra and the intentional act of speaking truth at all times.

Another realization during this step in my yoga journey happened when I realized I hold family and tribal tension in my hips. This is associated most closely — though not solely — with guilt and aligns with the spleen chakra. Energetic therapy for this would address trust and the ability to feel and to be present and intimate.

Yoga practice taught me to release the tension in my lower back. My emotional work through yoga brought me to awareness that in my back I was working to establish and maintain positive self-worth. This is associated most closely — though not solely — with sadness or failure and resides in the solar plexus chakra. Energetic therapy for this would address the ability to celebrate or take pride in my identity and accomplishments.

Motivated by my life situation, I came to this awareness with the help of others and by self-work. It's not easy to find a curriculum for self-integration, yet yoga brings us to a heightened awareness and raises the beginning steps for emotional healing as the yogi's ongoing project.

Our lives carry imprints of physical injuries, emotional blocks, and failure; but there's much more. Through yoga, we connect to our true selves and then we begin to reshape negative imprints. Depth psychology asserts that our bodies and minds carry imprints of physical injuries, emotional blocks, and failures; but it doesn't end there. The physical and emotional therapy of yoga begins there.

A yoga song for transforming the emotional body is Bob Marley's "Redemption Song." "None but ourselves can free our minds," he wrote. In yoga, we respond to the yoga song that our body is singing, and since we occupy the best position to define and transform our emotions, we use this knowledge to rewire our lives and release negatives when getting in touch with our emotional bodies. Yoga teachers could also rightly say your yoga song might bring some emotions out of you that you were not yet ready to receive. But this is how the growth curve works, we may not be quite ready but are pushed by the emotion and physicality of yoga into the next bend on our journey.

Recently a friend went to a Carlos Santana concert. He wrote that it was "a spiritual experience." I asked what he meant by that, and he responded. "Music always moves me, but his words were filled with grace and love; the mixture of children's photos throughout the world smiling and dancing. He issued a call to "rise up" above the hatred. The music just echoed the experience. It went deep with me!"

It's no surprise to hear that music does this; it's also what the yoga song of your body does in practice. Yoga, like music, is a visual, emotional, acoustic, vibrational, and feeling based experience in the moment. It goes deep, and when the yogi listens to the yoga song of their own body, yoga takes them to work on transforming the emotional body and vice versa. It may very well lead to engaging a professional therapist because through yoga many emotions arise from the deep well of biological and cerebral memory.

Our working ground is the yoga mat and self-reflection happens in time. When the yogi practices and reflects, healing happens in remarkable stages. All it takes is the yogi's attention to the emotions of the body, which leads them, like music, to go deep and transform the emotions that truly hold the steering wheel of form and function.

Chapter 18

Truth Force in Your Yoga

When practicing yoga, we tune-up mind, body, and spirit; this practice in self-care prepares us to serve when and where we are able. Preparation for life and service take place on the mat, a place that is sacred space. I like to call it the container within the container.

If you do yoga, you've noticed how teachers remind you to stay on the mat. "On your mat the magic takes place," one of my teachers said. At the beginning of class, we embrace a space on the yoga mat. This helps us shrink the unmanageable world if only for a short time.

Recently, I saw a person repeatedly stepping off and on the mat in class. I remembered watching a track athlete just before the race when they walk away from the starting line for a moment and circle around to calm their nerves or psych themselves up. Our first challenge in class is to stay in place, which means staying present on the mat to experience the full truth force rising from an intentional self-encounter.

Yoga is different from athletics through, because we are not competing; rather, we are engaged in encounter with self. I call it a martial art of the soul. This important encounter takes place as we embody asana, mobilize prana through breath, surrender our cares, and slow the busy mind.

On my second trip to India, I studied at the Gandhi Peace Foundation in New Delhi and talked with Gandhian scholars from around the world. In the center's library I read of Gandhi's *Jan Path*, a way of living anchored in truth force (*satyagraha*) and his philosophies of bread labor for individual and communal wholeness to sustain local economies. It's is a wholesome and selfless program of local community service;

healthy diet, meditation, cleanliness for body, economic justice, care for community, children, the infirm, family, and for the nation-state.

Yoga's complete program – one including all the limbs of its teaching — moves us to appreciate many of these same values and choices. We learn this through our yoga-study and the revelation of our deepest truths. When we stay on the mat in yoga, a container within the container, we discover another level of identity and a broader revelation of truth force. Staying present in the container awakens within us a satyagraha.

This force brings about a slow but certain alignment of body and soul, and while staying on the mat looks to others like a task, it's much more. It's a crucible in which we find freedom through structure, and truth through commitment to Self.

Not long ago, I watched a video of two men attempting to release a wildcat from a trap. One of the animal's legs was caught in its iron jaws, but since it had sharp teeth and claws, the men were cautious as they tried to pin it down so they could set it free. The big cat was aggressive and panicked, but eventually it tired and they were able to wrestle it to the ground and free the cat from the trap.

Sometimes on our yoga mat, we may experience panic like the big cat; there are moments when our bodies shake, and our minds race with doubt. As we stay on the mat during stress, we learn to breathe in ease where we find comfort and stillness in the midst of stress. This is yoga's marvelous therapy and a necessary antidote in today's high stress world.

Yogic awareness leads to acceptance of our experience. But it's a conscious acceptance, for we ask: Am I fully here?, how are my mind and body responding?, am I enjoying this?, am I cursing or praying?, submitting or resisting?

The answers are private and specific to us, yet the force of yoga truth teaches us to be still and live a new way measured by new dimensions. It levels our judgments and brings us to the healing ground of calm detachment while simultaneously counseling us through its behavioral and moral observances (*yamas* and *niyamas*) to say and do the right things.

In the pressured spaces of post-Modernism and its perilous stress, yoga moves us to meet a difficult world and greet it with equanimity. Yoga's song teaches us to expand the dimensions in which we live and move and so we practice, study, and seek to discover who we are.

Yoga's truth force brings us to face ourselves on our yoga mat. We fall back into the fullness of Self where lessons of motion and stillness teach us to extend our range of motion, deepen our breath, fill our lungs, lengthen our stretch of spine, and grow the reach of our limbs in space. Living the truth force of yoga's spiritual science we breathe deeply, and in that breath, release and enter the realm of our lived experience on the mat; an experience strengthened by the force of truth with ourselves first, and then others.

Yoga, formed from the crucible of scholarship and body, mind, and spirit intention, will empty and then fill the thinking reed that is the human being. It redeems scapegoats and embraces the full panorama of humanity in all its races, colors, and identities.

Yogis then join a long line of grateful beings stepping into a parade made of kings and queens. In yoga, many are yoked together as one in union (*yuj*). In the yoga community, we are one on our mat in breathcentric practice, but we are also a corporate group together as one. We are singular, and also one global community; slowly cleansed and restored into a new creation by the old song of an eternal melody.

All the questions teach us to still the clash between adrenalin — stress — and relaxation or ease. We train with breath-work to handle panic moments, and we experience a freedom that comes after complete surrender to the moment as it was with the trapped wildcat.

Off the mat, yogis read, study, and shape their lives in order to receive the gifts of yoga and its lifelong benefits. On the mat, the yogi opens the door to the truth force of an ancient healing practice.

Truth force is the natural and predictable outcome from yoga's design and we discover this satyagraha by staying on the mat and experiencing the full intention, translation, and application of yoga to our lives.

When we stay with yoga as a life-long encounter with truth force, an ongoing song opens us to cues from within and without. Paying attention to these cues and the Jan Path of personal transformation, we will find truth force permeates our being and opens up the cold, steel traps that bind.

Chapter 19

Ritual Process and the Yogi's New Song

Much is written about ritual and its symbols. Taking note of yoga's ritual space helps us appreciate a fuller story of our yoga and the function of places where we practice. Today, most of us drive to a studio and then step over a threshold and into a room with four walls.

Moving into that space is the first action in a therapeutic process that's far less stringent than the history of yoga might suggest, when yoga goals included the achievement of immortality or living in absolute freedom. Ritual studies (the examination of how cultural rituals work), calls the step over a threshold into a specific place, a submission.

Scholars propose there are at least three steps in a process of transformation: submission, containment, and enactment. A starting point in ritual submission is the submission, including a willing surrender of control.

In settings where strong discipline drives the submission, the student arrives to a container at the appointed hour and often given new identity markers like clothing, haircuts, or pledges; and then immersed into structured rituals such as group meals, classes, and exercises.

This step is frequently a clear separation from previous life and into the rituals of initiation. The recruit's ego may not be broken, but they will form to submission. There's a great deal of peer pressure in such a process, and this peer pressure – or sense of belonging – brings all but the most independent persons to submission.

Psychologists tell us there are three key aspects in a personal identity, and a large part of this identity serves to amplify the process of submission through the comfort of belonging. First, when joining a group, everyone asks: who's here; second they want to know who's in charge; and finally their question is how they fit in to the group.

These questions are quickly an unambiguously answered for the recruit going through the submission process. They are provided with rewards as motivation, and slowly shaped to inhabit their new roles and cast off old identities.

In yoga, however, the submission process is voluntary. Separation from one's old life is usually temporary — often just an hour at a time — but as the yoga student submits to the ritual process, they join others in a common identity as students.

During the process of containment, some groups assign rank or titles, but yogis dispenses with rank and everyone is invited to release distracting personal issues, concerns, or worries. In the containment space like a practice room, yogis leave personal property and artifacts outside. In that way, yogis submit to entering the activities within a container, but they focus on who they are in the moment without the shadow of social roles interfering in the process.

At a Hawaiian yoga studio I attended, a sign on the door separated the ritual container from the world and reminded yogis that on the other side of the door was a place set apart.

This is a SACRED SPACE

We kindly ask…

RESPECT

The silence of the room

AVOID

Complaining and cursing

HONOR

Positive atmosphere and healing

-Namaste

Within the ritual container, the space is sacred training ground. Although the demands on the yogi are not as extreme as in the military or some other groups, yogis are focused when they cross a threshold, step into the container, and begin ritual posture with breath and meditation.

The container often formalizes increased physical demands while the yogi works on endurance, concentration, and balance. Containment and ritual work become a combined power, magnifying focus and removing distractions from the room. All of this serves to center the yogi's attention during their important yoga moments.

A yogi is not required to stay in the container, but they willingly stay because they believe the container provides healing. The yogi hears unified and steady breathing from other initiates and they may embody a posture of prayer with hands folded at heart center. They experience moments to let go, chant Om (A-U-M), or meditate upon the sound of music, a bell, or some other sound signaling the conclusion of class.

The yoga room is sacred space and yogis remove their shoes to signal they know it too. I also am open to transforming moments, minor miracles, or perhaps a mystical encounter, which is referred to in religion as direct experience with God. But neither the yogi nor the recruit can remain in the ritual container. They must cross back over the threshold and return to lives on the outside where they enact new thinking and being in their life off the mat.

Containment is the second act in the yogi ritual process. It's built upon the skills they learn by entering the container in submission. For a yogi in ritual process, learning and development accelerates inside the container due to the nature of focus and attention to the moment. If it's a safe space, and if a yogi is dedicated, the second step in ritual process works like a pressure cooker speeding everything up even when it appears to move slowly.

Meanwhile, the yogi's insights from their work in sacred space often lead to personal change. Yoga may alter the yogi's future because they will make decisions based on an emerging identity and fresh values. Professionally, the yogi will most likely remain as they are or choose a new path.

A new path, even if it disrupts a life that people view as successful, doesn't mean you've ruined your current life; but it likely will change your priorities and raise new questions about it. This is how ritual process brings elements of our lives front and center, and perhaps even forces us to pay attention and grow. We learn there are many seas to sail and many ways to live; but we also learn that we are the captain of our own ship.

Think of a yogi in the container during the course of several months. If they've had an experience with a ritual teacher of integrity in an effective and safe container; and if the yogi is faithful to do their yoga, the yoga ritual will do its work in the process of transformation.

Remember the sign on the Hawaiian yoga studio's door to the container? This (container) is a sacred space . . . respect and honor please. That's what happens in the container, the yogi learns respect and honor for themselves, for the yoga song they enact, and for others.

Enactment, the third stage in a ritual process of transformation begins when and if the yogi starts making changes in their lives: altering or modifying their diet, refining their habits, prayers, or careers; they may spend more time with new people, or less time with other friends, or studying new ways of being and living.

Maybe the yogi's enactment of new learning will open them to new forms of music; they might begin exploring creative endeavors and new art. Small changes happen easily, but small changes lead to bigger changes and the yogi might think about making big life decisions like shifting careers or moving to another country.

Enacting these changes in life might be difficult for others to understand and accept; and some watching from a distance might say the yogi has ruined his/her life, but if the yogi is led to enact their new vision they will grow stronger and the importance of others' opinions will fade.

Enactment into a new identity involves some risk and interruption of the standard way of being, but when one mends broken wings, and becomes strong in the broken places, they will charter a flight to new courses and find new landings. The yogi might have to plan, sacrifice, and experience uncomfortable days, but they will be whole and they will be authentic.

And once these three stages are completed, the yogi might be described – in the words of an old farm saying – as a "thump-ripe melon"; sweet and messy, with a refined personal identity built on a yoga song formed in the ritual container of change.

Chapter 20

Release into Savasana

Silence . . . it doesn't seem like such a tall countercultural order, but think of the last time you were in a group of silent people. It happens rarely; and for some, quiet is so unnerving they actually feel unnatural in silence. It's a strange paradox that a quiet outdoor setting has become, for some, a scary venue. This is why I believe silence and quiet both within and without is one of yoga's overlooked benefits.

Normally during yoga class only the teacher speaks. Other yogis are present, but are asked to remain quiet and taught to breathe through their noses. The artifacts of our professional lives are left outside the container: costumes, jewelry, phones, and shoes are not in the yoga space. Some classes offer music, but talking is stilled.

Social talk is welcome before and after class but during class everyone is relieved from the expectation to speak or to appear happy, or witty, or social. Gathered yogis give-in to the refreshing and sometimes uncomfortable stillness of not talking. At times, the song of silence is the most potent song.

Teachers use the term "pacing" when talking about presenting new material in a classroom. Pacing is built on the idea that it's important to build-in time for the mind and body to digest new information or experience. This requires that the teacher stop talking for a moment so students can catch up, to process and digest what they've heard. It's almost as if time slows when the mind has time to ruminate on new information rather than rushing to catch-up or listen to the next thing. Stillness and quiet may be the most important seconds in both education and yoga as we allow quietness to wash-over the noisy cacophony of daily commerce.

Corpse Pose (*savasana)* is a time during yoga class when yogis may find stillness, quiet, and new learning. In the quiet of savasana, time seems to slow because we're giving ourselves a mental and physical break. In savasana, yogis have a space to slow down and truly sink into the ground. Nothing else is required. For some it's the most difficult asana.

Savasana also gives our ears a break, and the minutes of savasana allow for anything but business as usual. At the end of a class, I came to a new insight when the teacher said, "Release into savasana."

The statement was a fresh way for me to hear not only how to prepare for the end of a yoga session, but in a larger sense, the end of life. If savasana is meant to be a precursor to our bodies in death, then we <u>are</u> metaphorically dead in the savasana pose.

Ernst Becker wrote about this in *Denial of Death*, positing that most of us do not want to think about our death. In savasana, we are given a brief moment to do just that; to contemplate the day when the only thing between us as a real corpse, and ourselves in savasana pose, is our breath.

Many of us long for a place to release our grip — and we desperately need moments when noise from within and without dissolves — we thirst for moments to be free from our ego and its grasp. Releasing into savasana is our moment of relinquishment, and in that moment, we can release our ego-investments and obsessions shaped by old-fashioned hierarchical structures.

Savasana looks unimpressive. It appears easy when yogis lie on their backs while surrendering both talk and movement. Corpse pose impacts each yogi in unique ways and is often deeply personal. For some, it is the biggest challenge in a yoga class.

In savasana, we have the perfect time to remember the idea of pacing. The next time you are in savasana, take an extra moment to let the new learning in your body catch up to you. Remain present in silence, let time slow, and take a moment to contemplate your demise rather than deny it.

Yoga is partially about finding a space to break from mental storms. We can step back from the outer image we construct and project to the world and "release into savasana." For some, silence and contemplation may not happen in yoga, but in nature and on the banks of a mountain stream gurgling out a soft song; others may find ease resting in grass next to a stack of cordwood, or sunbathing on Hawaiian black volcanic rocks, listening to the Pacific Ocean's soothing tide-song.

In *Living Your Yoga*, Judith Hanson Lasater writes of how savasana taught her to dis-identify from mental storms and go within. "I learned to recognize more quickly when I had abandoned the present moment once again, and I learned not to judge myself when I had done it for the millionth time, and not to dance away so quickly with my thoughts."

In a larger sense, releasing means to loosen my grip. And the more I meditate on savasana, the more I realize that I — and maybe you — hold tightly to life and its demands. Yes, it's important to get a grip on our lives, but it doesn't have to be a stranglehold. Releasing our tight grip on things (*aparigraha*) is part of yoga's wise counsel in the yamas. One translation of aparigraha reads as "not seizing." In savasana we are released from the temptation to grab for more and released from the temptation to reach out and seize more.

As we temporarily release into savasana, we are offered time and space to contemplate our final release. Set free from grasping, gripping, and seizing, we release into savasana and inherit yoga's gift.

Chapter 21

Armor On, Armor Off: the psychology of yin yoga

To an outside observer yin yoga looks simple; yet it's anything but simple. It's deceptively hard; people appear to be sleeping, or basking in repose to catch their breath for something that might happen later. Something *is* happening, but it's not sleep; neither is it warm-up for a vigorous series that might follow.

To Americans enamored by action, action, and more action, a group of people engaged in rest and reflection seems like a waste of time. Yin yoga might remind them of preschool or kindergarten when the nap took place just after milk and cookies. But the process of yin yoga leads to complete inner opening, which takes time to fully experience and understand.

When I started yin, teachers directed me to release muscular control and find bodily support by use of props. At first, I thought it was easy too. They said we were doing good work and were easing out of muscular control so the fascia tissue in our bodies could engage slow, careful stretches. I wanted to know more about fascia so I started by researching articles on Dr. Russell Schierling's "*Fascia Superpost.*"

I found good information there, but I needed to experience it too. I continued reading and practicing yin for several months and thought I was doing what I needed with muscular release and letting the fascia slowly expand.

I came to understand that the challenge in yin is mental and psychological. The foundational principle in yin yoga is relinquishment and surrender, the key to yin yoga's psychology and morphology. Yin yoga is physical therapy through surrender, release, and relinquishment and its communication is internal.

Psychologically, surrender in yin yoga is the key to everything. Early on I thought I was surrendering and releasing muscular control, but there are so many levels to doing so that it took a long time before I understood the full impact of surrendering to the moment.

During my training as counselor and ritual leader, I read *Angel in Armor: A Post-Freudian Perspective on the Nature of Man.* Author Ernest Becker maintained that we go through life shouldering protective armor, and like knights of the Medieval Age, we carry this armor and clank around burdened by heavy protection. We rarely give up our armor for fear of being vulnerable. But heavy armor hinders our agility on mental, physical, and psychological levels.

Focusing on this loud and heavy outer shell as our protection, our attention scans outward to the environment and yet our vision is obstructed and obscured because our perception is not perfect, and because we are gazing through shielded armor, protective masks, and defensive postures against threats real or perceived.

This habitual looking-outward — and being-on-guard —hinders our ability to look inward. This is why yin is so hard; its focus is away from the exterior to the vulnerable and unprotected interior.

In yin, when one finally releases character armor and moves into a deeper point of release, one feels the stretch in a new way. Then it's easy to understand the psychology behind yin yoga because when one stretches deeper into the pose and feels sensation, the heavy armor we stubbornly cling to is cast aside as we inhabit a vulnerable place.

This is the great gift of yin. The deep release and flex take us to release and we lean into it. This does not happen in one session; but we return and revisit in order to let it go more and more. We don't ask for something to come forward; we only drop the protective armor for a minute, remain open, look inside, and wait for our unprotected being to begin the healing process, by de-armorizing.

To begin the healing process is to de-armorize. We may even come to the freeing and incredible realization that the angel — which is us — no longer needs armor. The tightness in the back, neck, jaw, shoulders, and front of body can be set at ease. Take a big breath and let it out slowly. That's what the practice of yin yoga and bodily healing feels like.

Then we come face to face with another principle of yin yoga, and that is trust. To trust the process, one must be open. This is frightening to us, for it means losing the armor; and without armor we are vulnerable.

It's difficult in our day because we are surrounded by a culture awash in threat and violence. If you need proof, turn on the nightly news for just a few minutes and observe how your armor goes up. A second place you can check your armor is in the car. Some day when you are driving and in a stressful situation, stop for a moment and notice where you are tight.

Most of us will do anything to avoid going inward; to be open, vulnerable, and trusting is rare. And this is why most of us run around like chickens without heads, consumed by action, action, and more action. This busyness is a way of distraction in a distracted culture; but yin yoga counsels us to look inward and let distractions go.

In The Yoga Sutras, Patanjali wrote of distraction in the second thread with the term *yogascittavrttinirodhah*. The counsel in this phrase tells the yogi to direct their mind and sustain their focus without distraction. It is learning to cease the activity of our monkey minds. In yin yoga, when we have time to deal with our monkey mind, time to let the whirlwind cease, time to let go from distraction in body and mind in order to feel and be present.

It's far easier to participate in a vigorous asana series than it is to release character armor and come home. But in yin we relearn that home is where the heart truly is; and if we've lived even for a short time, we know that where the heart is, heartache is also present.

When we take the armor off, even for a 60-minute yin yoga class, we enter healing territory. Relieved from the burden of carrying our protective shell, we touch something – in our bodies, minds, and fascia — something we are protecting. But its also something we may not want to discover.

Yin yoga invites us to take the armor off, to be the angel without protection, to release the stress, to drop the defenses. Yin gives time and space for us to turn the gaze inward, to open with surrender and trust to the heart of this healing. Give it time and trust that yin will heal the angel in armor by taking you beyond that which binds up fascia and burdens your heart with armor.

Chapter 22

First and Last Breath

The principles of breath management (pranayama) and breath training, teach that a breath executed in ease and awareness grounds our asana and our yoga, bringing us to a closer inspection of our lives and our mortality. Asana, without its integral relationship to pranayama, is still good exercise but yoga is much more than good exercise.

Yogis have been articulating the importance of pranayama for centuries. Once a person starts, it doesn't take long for them to realize yoga is a breathcentric practice that changes minds, bodies, and spirits.

Patanjali wrote, "Through the right control of breath, we overcome ignorance." Breath awareness is a hallmark of the yogi's identity, and breath management connects the yogi to the intimate biological process of breathing as the energy and imminent life force.

In America, the practice of pranayama is an important observance by itself, but often it's treated as an ancillary aspect to asana, as if a requisite attention given to breathing for five minutes at the beginning of class is sufficient warm-up for the real work of asana.

There are many approaches to the practice of pranayama in Western yoga; some start with pranayama before asana but this is often brief. Some focus on the technique of inhaling through the nose with a sound in the throat (*ujjayi*), throughout asana; some teachers pause the class to work on pranayama, and others might highlight pranayama as something to do near the end of practice.

But to more fully activate the vital life force central to the construction of our foundation and life, it's important to conduct breath work and pranayama as a distinct activity with its own benefits and techniques as well as a guiding anchor for life.

When teaching, I begin with a pranayama set and it's longer than what I experience in classes with others; it's not something I rush through in order to get to asana. A teacher in a class I attended recently said, "If you learn about breath in yoga, and how it can change our physiology and biology, you may not have to learn anything else." And during his first yoga class ever, an 80 year old man caught the same spirit. His replacement knees made it difficult for him to bend and his body ached, but he did the pranayama — practicing inhale and exhale -- while observing others doing asana. He couldn't execute the poses, but after class I heard him say to others, "It's all about the breathing. It's the most important thing."

Pranayama is the deliberate and conscious linking of breath with movement that sets yoga apart from other sports and disciplines. On occasion, there may be a brief pause or hold during asana, but with the inhale (*puraka),* exhale (*rechaka*), and the breath hold (*kumbhaka*); the yogi mobilizes prana. Nearly anyone can participate fully in a yoga class even if their breath is not integrated with asana.

We come into life through our most violent and important breath; we also leave this way when our breath – much weaker at the end – is exhaled one last time. "There is no asana without breath and no breath without asana," Iyengar wrote in *Light On Pranayama*. And in *The Heart of Yoga* T. K. V. Desichachar wrote, "Yoga is as much a practice involving breath as it is involving the body."

Explaining or defining prana is difficult. "It's as difficult to explain prana as it is to explain God," Iyengar wrote, and then went on to offer these thoughts on prana:

Prana is the vital energy of life.

Prana is the prime mover of all activity.

Prana is the hidden or potential energy in all beings.

Prana is energy which creates, protects, and destroys.

Prana is the energy permeating universe at all levels.

Prana is the principle of life, according to the Upanishads.

For its seeming centrality to the traditional masters, pranayama in contemporary practice tends to be overlooked. It isn't because teachers don't understand the importance of pranayama — they do — but because the Western standard of a one hour time block that most yoga classes fall into doesn't lend itself well to exploration of both pranayama and asana with any level of depth. A friend, whose mother teaches yoga in India, returned from visiting her recently and said, "in the classes I attended, we spent most of the time practicing pranayama."

When yogis arrive in class from lives of busyness, they are still on a fast track and primed to move and eager to keep going. I've noticed over time, that when yogis come to realize the importance of pranayama, they develop a willing attitude and are eager to engage in breath work.

Traditional practices included asana and pranayama as a unified set and both are necessary for yoga. A practical reason for doing both is that pranayama increases the expansive muscular power and opens up space for diaphragm movement within the rib cage.

Beyond the physical though, the deeper meaning of pranayama and asana as one activity is consistent with the Indian worldview of a unified field. India's belief system is capable of simultaneously holding two antitheses strongly marked, and it comes to us in a philosophy of yoga that has incorporated both the cosmic and the psychic as one.

In *Yoga: A Scientific Evaluation*, Kavoor T. Behan wrote, "The most important step in the development of Indian philosophy was taken when the brahman, the cosmic principle, and atman, the psychic principle in man were looked at as identical. This identity is briefly expressed by the saying, "That art thou" (*Tat tvam asi*); and "I am Brahman" (*Aham brahmasmi*)."

Our lungs capacity can expand to access more oxygen with practice, and by doing so, the body is better prepared for asana. Stig Avall Severinsen, one time world record freediver with a 20 minute breath hold, wrote in *Breatheology: the art of conscious breathing*, "When our breathing is calm and restrained, the mind relaxes. It is this trinity of heart, brain, and breath that you must bear in mind, since it is the source of your well-being and health."

Severinsen believes anyone can increase the vital capacity of their lungs and cites research showing to what degree this capacity typically declines with age. Our lungs are capable of holding approximately 3 liters of oxygen for women and 4 liters for men in their 30's. By the time we live to 80, that capacity decreases to 1.5 for women and 2.8 for men.

But with pranayama practice and exercises in breath holding, we may expand our vital lung capacity, adding volume to our total capacity. "There is a direct correlation between the vital lung capacity and health, so the better the lungs are utilized, the better you will become – even during an illness," Severinsen wrote.

One day after a strenuous yoga class, I heard a voice in my head telling me, the phenomenology of the wind is a poem; a poem is a temple, and a temple is a breath. I realized that a single breath is the temple of life and the genesis of all; everything goes back to the first breath and on to the last breath.

A focus on pranayama is yoga's connection to everything; and as we mobilize prana we also connect with the spiritual center of our dwelling. With our final breath, our prayer, we exhale the vital life force from our heart, the center from which we sing our yoga song; and the last breath, before we pass this world, is our complete release into gratitude for the song we sang and for the life we have lived.

Namaste

Chapter 23

A Yoga Song for All Beings

Yogis speak of the third eye, or head's crown, as a portal to access higher levels of consciousness. Accessing these higher levels has allowed some yogis to demonstrate physical feats that have been - through the centuries - the envy of India's workers in the material and visible world: magicians, jadoowallahs, and jinns.

Most of us are not expecting yoga to help us perform miraculous works; we're happy when yoga helps us to meet a stressful world and greet it with equanimity. In today's yoga, we practice, study, and breathe deep to inherit its spiritual science.

With each breath, we learn to let our body and mind release and enter the realm of Om, the universal vibration creating, animating, and redeeming everything by absorbing it all into its cosmic center, the heartbeat of all being. Yoga's grace is that it teaches us that we are connected to the ground of being that is holy at its core, and this core is the place from where it becomes a redemption song. On the journey, we follow yoga's compass pointing us to Om and it brings us home.

As yoga leads us to deepen our range of motion we learn to expand our lungs in breath, increase our stretch of spine, and extend the reach of our limbs in space. Its song comes to us in voice, chant, or in the powerful sound of a group together in a deep exhale.

Yoga is formed in the crucible of scholarship and exercise. Its methodology is to first empty, and then fill the thinking reed that is human. In this emptying out and refilling, yoga teaches us to be still and leads us step by step to inhabit fresh dimensions of existence.

In time, yoga levels our judgments and brings us to the healing ground of calm detachment while simultaneously counseling us through the yamas and niyamas to say and do the right things.

As grateful beings, we follow the threads of yoga and step out to create a parade of kings and queens; a parade that redeems scapegoats and embraces the full panorama of humanity in all its races, colors, and identities.

Yoga is for all — this is not ambiguous – therefore our yoga song sings a melody of inclusion, it's a procession yoking many together in union where all are cleansed and restored to a new creation by an old song of an eternal melody.

It's hard to explain yoga to the uninformed, and it's hard to explain the supernatural too; so we draw upon metaphor because we can't describe direct experience with something that we may not clearly see. However, it is easy to see brokenness and weakness in the material realm. We know what it looks like and we know what it feels like because we know how failure and brokenness feels. Rumi makes real the gravity of materiality. "You are an empty wine glass, I am granite. You know what happens when we touch."

You are not an empty wine glass, and I am not granite; but in life we learn what it's like when something like granite strikes glass. Yoga's journey, the melding of matter and mind, is the work of reassembling broken fragments of the material realm.

Yoga philosophy states that God exists within each human as atman. The atman and brahman within each human is the meeting of the universal principle and the individual. In yoga, the human and divine are soldered together, and the broken shards are reassembled in the yogi as a sacred being, present and perfectly completely here and now. This proclamation for the yogi means one is at union with the eternal now; in the present tense, it means that divinity is within. We are a melded union of divine and human in spirit and matter.

Spiritual perspectives require the task of mental discrimination, and part of that is a clear distinction between the notions of God as everything (*pantheism*) or God in all (*pan-en-theism*). This is the careful distinction to make regarding divinity.

If God is in (*en*) the essence of all matter and being, then divinity is in all beings. This is how to view atman. God is in the atman, and the atman is in all people. I would even state that the atman is in the essence of all beings.

Human ethics and morality become vastly more inclusive when the yogi embraces pan-en-theism, because then it means that I am not a god, but that the divine is in me just as it is in all sentient beings. This perspective raises the playing field to a level of divine respect for all things because God is in all things.

Gandhi once said that his creed of nonviolence is a very active force. This is not passive, but an unambiguous statement of an active, inclusive, respectful, and non-violent ethic. In the notion of satyagraha, there is no room for nationalism or racism; and violence is not acceptable because the divine is in all.

In *Anam Cara: A book of Celtic Wisdom*, John O'Donohue writes, "The eternal world and the mortal world are not parallel; rather, they are fused. The beautiful Gaelic phrase, *fighte fuaighte*, woven into and through each other, captures this."

Yoga answers the search for God by stating that we are one with divine essence. To know this is to take a step toward a higher consciousness, it's to inhabit a new kind of being, to relate with others from a posture of respect in healing and service. Like all conscious awareness and action, it starts with the self.

We sense in our yoga that something is happening beyond stretching and breathing. We may go to a yoga class and follow instructions while moving deeper into longing. This brings us home to the grace of our true divinity and humanity.

And while the roots of avidya are deep in humans, and human faults are well developed and far reaching, the practice of mindful yoga connects each of us to a redemption song, a yoga song. It's a song for everyone and it's the yoga song in everyone.

Epilogue

Yoga Song is not a scholarly treatment of ancient texts or a detailed study of yoga's historical variations with schools, histories, practices, religiosities, and gurus; such a study would require intense academic abilities in linguistics, theology, sociology, history, medicine, and mythology. My hope is that I have expressed through lyric narrative that yoga is a song within us, and in our practice of yoga, we are singing our yoga song.

I've aimed to articulate my experience of yoga as a physical, non-physical, and metaphysical therapeutic. To that end, I return to dimensions in time and space where yoga first tumbled me, and find myself back to the place where it started. I sing a new song and find myself at home. In the words of T.S. Eliot:

"We shall not cease from exploring

and then end of all our exploring

will be to arrive where we started

and know the place for the first time

. . .

And the children in the apple-tree

not known, because not looked for

but heard, half-heard, in the stillness

between two waves of the sea."

Many years ago, and far from the waters of Hawaii where yoga first tumbled me, I set out on a solo three-day vision quest in a barren land that Wyoming residents call the Red Desert. Before my quest began, I spent two days training in the Lakota way. Once I walked into the desert I would not eat or see anyone. My instructions were simple and focused: drink water and pay attention. For yoga, I'd give the same instruction today, only adding an admonition to breathe. I expected my vision quest would challenge me but also help me connect to that which I had not yet connected. I didn't know it, but at the time I was doing the work of yoga.

At dawn on the scheduled day, I walked into the desert to seek a new vision. My intention was to strip away all distraction in my experiment with truth and give it my full attention with all my being. This is what yoga is to me now. It's a stripping away of distraction, which takes preparation and intention. It is the time and place where I build my satyagraha.

In the Red Desert, I learned from the birds that if I had a song to sing I had to sing it. It was not about how well I sang, but that I did. This is why I've written *Yoga Song*; it is not about how well I write or sing my yoga song, but that I do.

Like most Western yogis, my practice draws only a small amount from the deep well of yoga's healing waters. I've inherited hatha yoga, a practice of equal and opposite forces in action. This does not make me an expert in yoga; rather, it opens me to become a seeker for the meaning of my forceful encounter with yoga that puts the dance between matter and consciousness front and center. My response as yogi, the sacred seeker to the sacred center, is to treat my yoga encounter as I to Thou, my martial art of the soul.

There are no rules about what a yogi must accomplish, but when the yogi is present, the yoking experience takes place in multiple dimensions. I believe every yogi experiences on conscious and unconscious levels both the heard and unheard, seen and unseen, felt and not felt.

When I am present in my yoga, I receive it in gratitude. This stands as the truth of my experience: a seeker, a yogi, a humble warrior in gratitude for every song.

A Six Point Yoga Precis

1. The yogi starts any session with gentle release and submission to the process. The ritual of yoga moves the yogi to enter a state of intentional presence.

The yoga world knows this as TRUST. In relinquishment, the yogi learns to open their heart and settle into the most important moment - - the one they live. This grounding in the present enables the yogi to engage themselves at deeper levels for conscious contact with self. This opens them to engage the reality of their life. Surrendering into the moment, the yogi experiences their life without filters. This is associative living, not escapist. The move to trust is a lived symbolism, for the yogi simultaneously participates in their life while pointing beyond it.

2. The yogi comes home to their breath-centric core where they kiss the soul to receive their full inheritance.

The yoga world knows this as BREATH. At the center point, breath is the building of consciousness. In heightened consciousness, jettisoning old scripts, the yogi constructs a personal story of renewal formed by inspiration. They learn their healing treasure is at the end of a long journey.

3. Asana and pranayama bring the yogi to a sacramental remembering of self. This transforms both the seen and the seer.

The yoga world knows this as EMBODIMENT. Yoga's alchemy, formed by movement and breath, is *anamnesis* connecting action and memory. The yogi lives into a sacramental dimension of existence by remembering – in each moment – their being-ness as both immanent and transcendent.

4. A path to community opens with the relinquishment of armor in a shared experience

The yoga world knows this as COMMUNITY.

Inside the yoga room, the awakened center is tutored in self-love and love for others. When vital energy and passion are shared, the body (individual and corporate) is fed by pranayama. Where there are no hierarchies, questions of worthiness are tossed out the window. There is no rank, systems, or bureaucracy. The yogi joins as a witness to one common identify - which points them back to an intimate connection with all.

5. The target of yoga's missiology is self.

The yoga world knows this as PRACTICE. In the container, at the confluence of yogi, guru, and healing practice, a drop of sweat takes one to self and self to God. The yogi – a vessel devoid of armor and ego - incarnates a healing curriculum in a generative engagement translated to a focused biology of belief and concomitant mind/body/spirit reshaping.

6. In savasana, space and time welcome the yogi for an anointing to the goodness of true self and true nature.

The yoga world knows this as HEALING. Yoga's internal *tapas* (heat of transformation) teaches compassion for self; in savasana's moments of rest, the yogi is anointed in yoga's healing tradition. This is not a cosmetic make over, but a weaving together of a timeless process which synthesizes everything up to that moment in a deep affirmation of life itself. By a second, yet deeper release into savasana, yoga's physical, non-physical, and metaphysical medicine works its healing therapeutic on the human.

Glossary

Ahimsa – the principle of non-harm or nonviolence to all living creatures. This is the first teaching of the *yamas*; the second is truthfulness (Satyagraha).

Atman – God within, the creative or real Self, the original breath, the imperishable self.

Patanjali believed that Atman has its separate but equal Brahman. The Atman is intelligence itself and the human reflects the Atman's eternally unchanging reality.

Bhagavad Gita – a philosophical text composed between 400 – 300 B.C., The text records dialogues between the Hindu God Krishna and the warrior Arjuna on the warrior's code: selflessness, duty, devotion, and meditation.

Brahman – the Atman in its universal aspects. Atman and Brahman are one.

Hatha – Literally, force; but in modern yoga, it's the practice of asana, pranayama, and meditation broadly called yoga. Hatha in the wider sense is known as one particular branch of yoga.

Prana – the immanent and transcendent energy (God's energy) permeating the earth at all levels. Prana is equated with Atman, or the soul in the Upanishads.

Moksha – meaning liberation or release. In a final (or eschatological) sense, moksha means freedom from death and ultimately a union with Brahman.

Niyamas and ***Yamas*** — the private life and corporate behavioral guidelines and observances for a yogi; these include moral counsel and the admonition to external cleanliness and the cleanliness of internal organs through the practice of asana.

Om – Sanskrit for the most basic, natural and comprehensive of all sounds. To the devout Hindu, Om is the basic fact of the universe.

Patanjali – Scholar, writer, teacher, often called the 'father' of modern yoga. While not solely his work, Patanjali is credited with writing the *Yoga Sutras*, built on primary sources and translated into many languages around the world.

Prakrti – matter or physical element

Purusa – spirit or source of consciousness

Satyagraha- the force of truth as described by Gandhi achieved through non-violence and physical discipline. *Sat*, the Sanskrit for "truth."

Sutras – threads or aphorisms attributed to Patanjali collected over the course of 800 years from 400 B.C. to 400 A.D. These threads (brief sayings) extol the way of yoga and the virtues of the dedicated yogi. Sutra 1 reads: "This is the beginning of instruction in yoga."

Tapas – heat or ardor designating an ascetic and sustained approach in rituals of transformation.

Vedas – from *vid*, to know the sacred knowledge of scripture. Vedic texts, teaching aspects of Hinduism were composed roughly between 1500 B.C., and 400 B.C. Large portions of the early Vedas were hymns for religious occasions, similar to the Psalms of the Old Testament. Early yoga traditions included intense study of the Vedas and other books of spiritual import.

Upanishads – texts that developed after the Vedas (800 – 400 B.C.,) and were contemporary with the sutras. Upanishads focused on the supreme soul's nature, especially the equality of Brahman and Atman, and the doctrine of karma and rebirth. During the post-Upanishadic period, the Yoga Sutras took up the cause of yoga as a way to liberation and salvation.

Yoga – Commonly thought of in the West as a physical exercise designed to shape the yogi's body and mind. Vedic thought maintained yoga as a system designed to shepherd the yogi to liberation from earthly bonds and achieve union with Brahman. Westerners often mistake this esoteric goal as an advanced achievement; whereas, the yogi viewed liberation as surrender. Yoga, developed in pre-scientific India, framed its work as the exchange of energy within the body and a union of self (atman) with Brahman.

The actual word yoga can mean many things: to yoke, a method, an activity, a force, a style of meditation, or a disciplined system of study and dedication. Some call yoga the "science of religion." Yoga schools developed in four major branches, each with its unique emphasis: *Bhakti yoga* (devotion), *Karma yoga* (God-dedicated action), *Jnana yoga* (intellectual knowledge and discrimination), and Raja yoga (meditation).

www.ingramcontent.com/pod-product-compliance
Lightning Source LLC
Chambersburg PA
CBHW022159160726
48282CB00024B/253